IAN PEACOCK

Bankers: from Pillars to Pariahs

For: Aly

novum pro

This book is also available as e-book.

www.novum-publishing.co.uk

© 2018 novum publishing

ISBN 978-3-99064-269-6
Editing: Julie Hoyle, BA
Cover photo:
Beataaldridge | Dreamstime.com
Cover design, layout & typesetting:
novum publishing
Internal illustrations: David Miles,
Jing Yang and Gilberto Marcheggiano,
The Economic Journal,
123 (March), 1–37.
Author's photo: Ian Peacock

The images provided by the author have been printed in the highest possible quality.

www.novum-publishing.co.uk

Preface

Fifty years of changing banking has seen more good than bad.
Peter D. Hahn
Henry Grunfeld Professor of Banking.

In late 2008, after the nationalisation of Royal Bank of Scotland and substantial government assistance to Lloyds in its rescue of Halifax Bank of Scotland, I was requested to answer questions on bank bonuses before the House of Commons Treasury Select Committee (TSC). I was an aspiring academic with a recent PhD coincidently focused on corporate governance and remuneration, but also a former banker who had worked in commercial and investment banking and received bonuses. The hearing was televised and accessible globally and I supported the concept of bankers' bonuses; I received a good deal of hate mail from around the globe following, perhaps to no surprise with the amount of taxpayers' money going to rescue banks in the UK, USA, and much of Europe. Yet, a few listened as I got in some detail on why the existing bonus system didn't work: poorly structured, calibrated, governed with the wrong incentives. I also noted that, if executed correctly, the flexibility to not pay bonuses was a financial safeguard for challenged banks. The devil was in the detail.

The crisis and the continuing surfacing of incidents of poor behaviour at major and minor banks have resulted in much banking nostalgia and longing for those 'good ole banking days' of the 20th century with memories of banks as the "Pillars" of society in this book's title, but were they really? In these days of rapidly reducing numbers of bank branches, I often hear "it was so much easier to go in and speak with someone." Yet, early in my career, banks were largely open from '9-5' when I had a job to do, if not fewer hours, and I often needed to spend most of my lunch break queueing to deposit my pay cheque. If one ran out of cash on Thursday, you might as well forget lunch on Friday with its extra-long waits to get to the counter. Weekends could find closed branches, rare or no machines then, and no cash for a few days. Many businesses didn't take cards, too. To write a cheque, a cheque guarantee card was required and they didn't get young people very far. And if someone paid me by cheque, not only another wait on the queue but a further wait for clearing the funds. Instant payments were a dream. But there was a bank manager you could patiently wait for, often he listened (not many she), could give comfort, and perhaps offer sound, conservative, advice – if you had time. This book provides a balanced account of these shortfalls and benefits.

Banks and other providers of banking services of memory were also seen as more gentlemanly – because, well, they often didn't compete. Price competition was thought unsavoury, viewed as potentially unsafe, by the banks and their regulator. Was this widely known? I doubt it. If you paid an extra one per cent interest rate on your 25-year mortgage, it is similar to paying 25% more for your house. Was everyone really OK with that? I wasn't asked. Yet, there was comfort in the knowledge that if trouble arose you knew who to speak to – you just didn't know how much that degree of service cost and no one, not the banks, really did. I am grateful for author Ian Peacock's efforts to tell this story and explain how banking changed as competition and products evolved.

The first iPhone and its later banking apps coincided with fall of Northern Rock; banking apps and easy smart phone banking have become synonymous with the age of digital or remote banking (though we've had online banking since the 1998) and are blamed for the decline of the branch. This book tells the story of how the credit card in 1966 began the wave of credit decisions moving from branch to central office, from subjective and often personal decisions to computer approvals ... that was 52 years ago. The digital transformation of banking has been remarkably slow moving by that measure.

This book provides a great service in reviewing a half century of banking, in detail, both good and bad. The author takes us through many of the devilish details: The consolidation of many inefficiencies in the system, such as very high cost protected specialist firms; The many culture clashes involved in merging those firms' activities; and how regulators were involved well beyond what any law provided to their sudden loss of power and, finally, a massive increase in banking law and new regulators' powers. The subject nearest to my career about banking is that of culture, in banks, in banking businesses, building it and destroying it. Not many years before the financial crisis, a then lauded bank chairman who didn't come from banking publicly derided the conservativeness of his bankers and his bank's governance when he hired a non-bank trained CEO. That bank became the biggest bank failure of all time – its leaders followed me to answering questions before the TSC and a shocked nation; this book puts that failure in context.

Our Brexit referendum process raised many questions and one of my favourite issues to arise out of the referendum concerned how our views of the past influenced our views of the future of our country; I take no sides here and note that multiple views of the past were expressed. However, I hope this book's providing of greater clarification of banking past help us to better formulate banking future, based more on facts and important detail than nostalgia. I have wondered out-loud if our banking ring-fence regulation, which must be implemented next year, was about a nostalgic view of recreating a misunderstood past or about a better way forward. At a speech about ring-fence banking last year, a well-known economist told me that ring-fencing was about recreating a 1980s banking environment. I will leave readers to ponder the desirability of returning to the past as they read this valuable book.

Introduction

Bankers currently are regarded as people out for themselves who are besotted with greed and who seem incapable of judging risk. Yet a few decades ago bankers were regarded as pillars of society, if somewhat boring; people who were unlikely to cause a stir. Anthony Sampson could write in 1962[1] 'The puritan, nonconformist conscience of the early days still hangs over [the clearing banks].' How have the banks and the bankers themselves changed over the period and how has society helped to mould those changes? Is there any way in which, in a modern, open, global society, bankers can redeem themselves and begin to act responsibly in providing and being seen to provide a useful public service? This account will attempt to answer these questions in the context of the UK, recognising that UK market developments have been profoundly influenced by events elsewhere.

PART I

Chapter 1

The Situation in the 1950s and 1960s

The structure of banking in the 1950s and '60s was much as it had developed over a century earlier. At the apex was the Bank of England. The Bank exercised monetary policy using several different levers. According to the Radcliffe Report, published in 1959, the authorities had used the following measures to control the monetary aggregates: '... manipulation of short-term interest rates (but not of long ones); funding the floating debt, and so reducing the banks' liquidity; official guidance – and eventually the fixing of a ceiling – on bank advances; the restriction of capital [market] issues ... and hire-purchase regulations.'[2] These tools could be mandatory, for example, the controls on hire-purchase lending, but more frequently they involved 'persuasion' by the Bank – known as Governor's eyebrows. Bankers were expected to take note of the 'mood music' emanating from Threadneedle Street (the Bank's Head Office). This included the Bank Rate, which although it had real effects, was also a highly symbolic figure. Professor Cairncross while questioning Lord Cobbold (Governor of the Bank) for the Radcliffe Committee in 1959 noted that 'there is an old saying that prayers and incantations, with a little arsenic, will poison a flock of sheep. I wonder whether the Bank Rate plays the role of the incantations here.' The Committee concluded that an increase in Bank Rate without other measures such as controlling public spending or hire-purchase terms would be – in the Governor's phrase – like 'spitting into the wind.'[3]

The Bank also had two other pivotal roles in the financial system – it was the principal bank of issue of banknotes and, increasingly during the nineteenth century, it acted as a regulator of the banks, particularly after the failure of Overend, Gurney and Company in 1866. As noted by Niall Ferguson,[4] 'Walter Bagehot, reformulated the Bank's proper role in a crisis as the "lender of last resort" to lend freely, albeit at a penalty rate, to combat liquidity crises.' For the last 150 years, banks have been unusual in that, unlike other types of commercial organisation, they could expect to be funded by a central authority if they ran out of cash.

Beneath the Bank, the most potentially powerful institutions were the clearing banks. Following rapid consolidation in the nineteenth century, clearing banking became highly concentrated amongst a very few names. By 1962, around 80% of all bank deposits were in the 'Big Five' banks: Barclays, Midland, Lloyds, Westminster and National Provincial (Westminster and National Provincial merged in 1968). These banks traditionally provided individuals and society with five principal services. Banks acted as channels for monetary transactions; retail suppliers of currency; trusted depositories for surplus funds; a mechanism for transforming (largely short term) deposits into (generally longer term) loans and a process whereby credit is allocated to those who are deemed worthy of receiving that credit.

These services are absolutely essential to the proper day to day running of an advanced economy. In 2015, the Greek authorities announced that banks would be closed for a week and that the availability of notes through ATMs would be limited. In fact, the banks were closed for three weeks. It is unlikely that much longer period of closure is compatible with the operation of commerce. Within a few days, people begin to hoard currency and banknotes become short. It becomes increasingly difficult to transact normal day to day transactions for food, fuel and clothing. And it becomes obvious that banks are utilities, in the sense that they perform a vital public service. This was recognised by the UK Government during the 2008 crisis and those banks seen to be in trouble were rapidly and publicly rescued.

By the nineteen sixties, the UK banking system was orderly, though hardly competitive. From 1939 until 1958, as Anthony

Sampson points out[5], the Treasury restricted overdrafts and the banks agreed amongst themselves not to compete for lending business. There were some glimmerings of competition – Midland Bank opened a branch on the *Queen Mary* – but broadly the clearing banks put stability and trust above competition and profits. Typically, banks kept 30%+ of their assets in liquid form[6] and lent for comparatively short periods, often at call but usually only up to 5 years maximum. Contrast the banks in the lead up to the 2008 credit crisis when banks' liquid assets went down to miniscule levels – well under 5% of their assets and they lent money for periods of 25 years and beyond.[7]

The banks also saw themselves as pillars of the social system, A colleague of mine, when he worked for Lloyds Bank, asked his manager for a mortgage (the servicing of which he could easily afford) for a detached house in Dorking. The manager refused on the grounds that it was a more expensive house than he, the manager, owned! More positively, bank managers saw themselves as trusted financial advisors to their customers. A letter to *The Times* provides a good example. Mr Broad (the writer of the letter) when young, some decades ago, had miscalculated his salary deposit and was called in by his Stourbridge bank manager. 'Mr Broad, you were £ 2 in the red last month, and £ 4 in the red this month. I'm afraid you appear to be someone living above his income.' (Letter to *The Times* June 15, 2015 from Ken Broad, quoting his Stourbridge bank manager's reaction to Mr Broad's 'miscalculating a salary deposit')

The archetypal banker could be as summed up by Anthony Sampson, 'In their dedication, their lack of greed, and their sense of quiet service, the joint stock bankers (i.e. the clearing bankers) provide a placid, safe centre to financial Britain.'

In truth, the banks were bankers to just one part of British society. The banks themselves were stuffy and rather off-putting to those who were not used to them. Banks were mainly for the middle classes, while majority of working men and women put their savings either into the Post Office or into mutually owned building societies. On 31 March 1961[8] the deposits in the Post

Office exceeded £ 6 billion, little different from the total deposits of the clearing banks. At the same date, deposits in those building societies which comprised the Building Societies Association were probably greater than those of the banks themselves[9]. The assets of these institutions differed from those of the banks. The Post Office was a mechanism for helping to fund the very large government debt which was a legacy of the Second World War. The building societies, as their name suggests, lent money to their members (who had usually been depositor members for a number of years) as mortgages for house purchase. At the time, the building societies had a virtual monopoly of the mortgage business, because banks were prohibited from mortgage business (apart from mortgages for members of staff). This may seem a strange restraint of trade but, given the problems banks later encountered when they were permitted to provide mortgage finance, perhaps there was some merit in it. It should be noted how risky the building society business model appeared to be. These organisations took short-term, often demand, deposits and lent the majority of them on mortgage for 30 years or sometimes longer. In principle, they appeared to be vulnerable to a run. Yet, there have been no significant defaults by building societies in which depositors have lost money (though there have been a number of 'guided' mergers). This has evidently been helped by the rise in residential property prices, but it was also helped by the 'club' atmosphere of the individual societies – they often drew members from particular localities or professions. Also, building society managers, who knew their borrowers well because they had usually been depositors for some time, were conservative people by inclination. As Sampson observes, 'The building society knights are earnest, moral men, who have seen a movement become an institution in their lifetime.'[10]

Another type of financial institution used increasingly by all sections of the population was the hire purchase (HP) company. These had sprung up in the nineteenth century to finance purchases of semi capital goods such as sewing machines. They were already evident in the pre-war economy. *The Spectator* reported in 1939, 'There seems to be no limit to the expansion of turnover which has been a feature of the history of the United Dominions Trust, the bank of which Mr J. Gibson Jarvie is chairman.' (United Dominions Trust being the largest HP company.) Nevertheless, at this stage they were comparatively 'small beer'. In the post-war society, customers became more reluctant to wait until they had saved enough to buy goods such as cars, televisions and refrigerators and the HP business grew accordingly. There were Acts of Parliament in 1938, 1954, 1957 and 1964 seeking to regulate this comparatively new market. By the late 1950s, HP debt was equivalent to around 30% of bank debt, and the HP business became impossible to ignore. Yet HP did not have a good name in some quarters. There was a view that people should save and only buy major goods with the fruits of that saving. Buying on the 'never-never' (as HP was known) was thought of as morally doubtful. These voices have not completely gone away as is evident from Joanne O'Connell's comment in *The Observer* Saturday 25 August 2012. Una Farrell, for the CCCS (Consumer Credit Counselling Service), says: "Hire purchase deals can sound great, and for some people they work. But if you lose your job you could end up in a situation where an interest-free deal ends before you've made a single instalment. The message,' she says, 'is that it's best to save up.' Ms Farrell's view was widespread in the 1950s and 1960s, particularly amongst more traditional bankers.

The institutions described above represented the vast majority of loans and deposits in the monetary system but there were other, often very influential, organisations which performed a range of specialised functions. For example, the Bank of England influenced interest rates by buying or selling bills of exchange and Treasury bills. In order to be 'eligible' for discount at the Bank, a bill of exchange had to be 'accepted' (i.e. guaranteed) by an organisation recognised by the Bank as an accepting house. These were the major merchant banks, numbering 17 organisations in 1962. The merchant banks carried out a number of other functions (including wholesale lending, money market and foreign exchange trading, bond issuance and dealing, equity issuance, corporate finance advice and investment management) but were named after their traditional bill accepting function. The merchant banks were not able to sell their accepted bills directly to the Bank of England. The bills were sold to a group of organisations called discount houses who in turn sold them to (or bought them from) the Bank.

None of the above entities dealt in equities. The merchant banks managed equity issues, i.e. flotations on the stock exchange and secondary market issues (i.e. issues of equity by quoted companies) and arranged underwriting for those issues. But the merchant banks neither sold equities to retail or wholesale buyers — this was the job of the stockbrokers — or traded in equities — the preserve of the stockjobbers. The merchant banks regarded themselves as superior to the brokers and jobbers (though there were also hierarchies within the broking and jobbing communities). In the mid-eighties, just before Big Bang, I was interviewing a merchant banker about the possibility of the merchant bank merging with a broker and a jobber (the law was about to change enabling such mergers to take place). He was against such mergers because 'broking was an insanitary business'. Such extreme views were rare but the feeling of a hierarchy of institutions definitely was not.

The highly specialised and formal institutional style had both advantages and disadvantages. Organisations tended to take notice of regulators' wishes, even when they did not have the force of law. For many years, the clearing banks agreed on a 'self-denying ordinance' under which they undertook not to compete with each other in the loans market.[11] I once fielded a call from the Bank of England (in the 1980s) requesting that we reduce the amount of a certain money market transaction on our books. The transaction was neither illegal nor ethically doubtful and we were breaking no regulatory rules, but it was having the effect of inflating the money supply, an indicator which the Bank then regarded as vital. We, of course, obeyed without question; the Bank had made its feelings known, so there was no alternative. Other organisations, such as the Takeover Panel, also usually operated by suasion rather than the force of law.

This behaviour towards regulators was part of a general concept of reasonableness. People worked hard in some areas of the City (not in others) and were generally paid well or very well, but not outrageously, for their efforts[12]. There was a feeling, whether justified or not, that fees, commissions, etc., while high, were not egregiously so.

A major problem with this cosy market was that many of the fees charged were essentially determined by cartel arrangements. For example, the accepting houses (the major merchant banks) used to earn a minimum of 1% p.a. when accepting (i.e. guaranteeing) short-term bills of exchange for blue chip borrowers. When British Petroleum broke this barrier and raised money at 7/8% p.a., the merchant banks were worried that their orderly world was threatened. These cartels did not of course encourage innovation, or excellence of any kind. 'In the 1950s and 1960s the British financial system was riddled with cartel arrangements, artificial distinctions and barriers'[13]. By the late fifties/early sixties there was pressure, both from within government and from the City itself, for some reform to take place.

Chapter 2

The Beginnings of Reform 1958–1970

Anthony Sampson in his *'Anatomy of Britain'* notes that in July 1958 'the "credit squeeze" was quite suddenly relaxed: the banks, to their astonishment, found themselves able to lend more money and they began competing.' Barclays took a stake in a hire-purchase company and Midland introduced a new form of personal loan. However, these were baby steps and in 1960 the Bank of England went into reverse by calling for 'special deposits' which constrained banks' ability to lend once more.

Through the 1960s there was relatively little change in the domestic role of banks. As pointed out by Pierce and Tysome,[14] special deposits became more formal and were extended to hire-purchase companies. The banking system remained uncompetitive, as observed in reports by the National Board for Prices and Incomes (1967) and the Monopolies Commission (1968). Banks had an agreement amongst themselves to fix deposit rates and minimum rates on loans. The discount houses had an agreement to buy up at an agreed price the weekly Treasury bill issue not sold elsewhere.

Yet, the London market was beginning to stir. As noted by Davies *et al.* in the Bank of England's Quarterly Bulletin, 'One of the most striking trends in this period [1962–1979] was the emergence of London as a truly international financial centre'.[15]

No one seems to know for sure the origins of the Eurodollar (and other Eurocurrency) markets. According to one account, the market began in 1956 when the Russian Government deposited dollars with Moscow Narodny Bank, which was London registered, fearing that deposits in New York banks might be confiscated by the US authorities in the wake of the unsuccessful Hungarian Revolution. Other versions attribute the origins to the Chinese Government and place the date in the late 1940s. Whatever the true explanation, the market was given a huge boost by the imposition of the US Interest Equalisation Tax (IET) in 1963. This measure, intended as a means of narrowing the US balance of payments deficit, imposed taxes on investments by US persons investing in foreign stocks and bonds. Its major unintended consequence was to encourage the holding of dollars in accounts outside the US. While the measure was repealed in 1974, by then the Euromarket had growth momentum and by 1978, US\$ 540 billion Eurodollars were booked offshore of the USA.[16] Eurodollar activity grew rapidly within UK and foreign owned banks and, during the 1960s and 1970s, a new type of bank, the consortium bank, was formed so that groups of foreign banks could 'club together' to participate in this burgeoning and exciting business. 'Between 1964 and 1971, seventeen consortium banks were formed from 110 partner institutions, of fourteen nationalities … By 1971, three of the seventeen consortium banks were located in Paris, one in Brussels, and the rest in London.'[17] Overall, the number of foreign bank branches and subsidiaries in London rose from around 50 to just under 130 between 1962 and 1970.

It may seem surprising that this new and more entrepreneurial market should have settled in London when the UK banks were so unenterprising (despite activity in Paris, Frankfurt, Geneva and other places, London became the undisputed centre of the Eurodollar market). The answer appears to be threefold. First, and most important, the UK had a regime which encouraged international capital flows, whereas the competing centres, such as Paris, discouraged these flows. Moreover, London did have a history of overseas financing partly, but not wholly, reflecting the importance of colonial trade. Some of the merchant banks had been active issuers of foreign bonds for many years – Baring Brothers began underwriting Buenos Aires Provincial bonds in 1824 and it was the underwriting of Buenos Aires Water Supply and Drainage Company Bonds which contributed to Baring's financial problems in 1890. Also, the clearing banks and other banks did have some experience of overseas business. In 1925, Barclays combined its 'imperial' businesses in Egypt, South Africa, the Caribbean and elsewhere to form Barclays (DCO), DCO standing for 'Dominion, Colonial and Overseas'. Lloyds Bank was a shareholder in, and later merged with, the Bank of London and South America. The British Bank of the Middle East was acquired by the Hongkong and Shanghai Banking Corporation in 1960. Finally, while the managements of the clearing banks may not have had a reputation for enterprise, some of the merchant banks, as their name suggests, were more forward looking.

The growth of the Euromarkets was associated with a range of new products and processes. The growth in the Eurodollar interbank trading enabled the development of the syndicated loans, and Certificate of Deposit and Floating Rate Note markets. 'It is generally accepted that the Eurobond market began with the Autostrada issue for the Italian motorway network in July 1963'[18]. The settlement of Eurobonds was facilitated by the formation of Euroclear in 1968 and other transactions by the setting up of SWIFT in 1973.

The other major change during the sixties was a domestic UK innovation – the launch of Barclaycard in 1966. Barclaycard retained an effective monopoly of the UK domestic credit card business until 1972 when a consortium of National Westminster Bank, Midland Bank, Lloyds Bank and the National & Commercial Banking Group introduced the Access card. Credit cards had two revolutionary implications. First, they changed consumers' spending behaviour: reducing the demand for cash and further eroding the traditional taboos against borrowing to buy consumer goods (see page 15). Perhaps more significantly for the development of the UK banking system, they changed the way in which consumer credit was assessed. Until credit cards were introduced, the local bank manager decided whether individual customers were 'good' for loans, i.e. were creditworthy. They decided this on the basis of personal knowledge of the customer as well as that customer's assets, liabilities, income and expenditure. No doubt the manager's own prejudices sometimes also played a part. The refusal by the Lloyds bank manager to grant a mortgage to his subordinate, quoted on page 13 is a, not unusual, example of those prejudices.

Barclaycard revolutionised this system and changed UK banking for ever. The Barclaycard company (which, according to a recent BBC Radio 4 programme, was distrusted and disowned by many Barclays branch managers) set out on a sales and marketing campaign and recruited salespeople from outside the banking sector. For example, Tony Russell, who was previously at Rothmans of Pall Mall, toured the country in a blue, white and gold suit with matching hat, accompanied by mini-skirted assistants. Prospective customers received one (or sometimes several) invitations to receive Barclaycards. The Bishop of Bedford was very displeased to receive three invitations, one addressed to Mr Bishop, another to Mr Bedford and the third to his actual surname.[19]

The introduction of the credit card enabled a further innovation, that of the modern ATM, the first of which in the UK was Lloyds Bank 'Cashpoint' in 1972 (though there had been a predecessor version launched by Barclays Bank at their Enfield branch in 1967). This was a great boon to the customer but of course it again diluted the personal link between bank teller and customer and reduced the need for tellers. In order to carry out their sales campaign, Barclaycard needed to decide which of their prospective customers was creditworthy. Interviewing everybody would have been a Herculean enterprise and, in any event, the cooperation of many branch managers would not have been forthcoming. The answer was credit scoring, a technique introduced from the USA. Instead of relying on the credit judgement of the bank manager, credit scoring looked at the measurable financial situation of the customer. The honesty and integrity of the customer was ignored, unless it could be measured (e.g. by looking at the number of court judgements against the customer). This system recognised that there would be a certain level of bad debts, but as long as this level was well below the level of profits it was regarded as acceptable.

Personal banking thus began to move away from the position where the bank manager endorsed the bank's customers to one where, as long as you fulfilled certain conditions, you were automatically eligible for a card. The role of the bank manager was thereby diminished and gradually over the years the influence, and later the number, of bank managers and their branches, gradually declined. The more automated approach, whether evidenced by 'holes in the wall' (ATMs) or credit scoring, ameliorated the problem which banks were finding with staff retention. It also had the advantage that groups who had found it difficult to get credit on their own account, notably women, could now be more financially independent.

Perhaps the most surprising aspect of the launch of Barclaycard was its haphazard nature. There was no business plan to speak of and the whole thing was done on the back of a six-page memo. Barclays paid a licence fee of £ 20,000 to Bank of America for their UK credit card franchise.

By the end of the 1960s, UK domestic banking practices and products had begun to change. The banks were becoming increasingly involved in the open and innovative Euromarket and at home, the close links between the manager and his customer were beginning to weaken. Yet the areas of competition and new products were a comparative rarity; banking was still a sector which was overwhelmingly controlled by anti–competitive rules and 'understandings'.

Chapter 3

"All Competition and no Credit Control"

Competition and Credit Control (CCC) was introduced by Anthony Barber, the new Heath Government's Chancellor of the Exchequer and became operative in September 1971. As pointed out by Zawadski[20], Competition and Credit Control had two principal aims: a) to ensure that the supply of financial resources is allocated to various uses by the free operation of the price mechanism (rather than, for example, by quotas) and b) to ensure that the authorities can ... exercise firm control over the size and the rate of growth of the stock of money. Under CCC, many of the cartels and formal links between interest rates were abolished and instead of special deposits being required from the banks, all financial institutions had to abide by 'Reserve Asset Ratios'. The clearing banks were for the first time able to conduct significant amounts of residential mortgage business.

The UK banks took the first point to heart. Competition broke out in the lending and deposit market and the clearing banks and other financial institutions competed actively on price and other factors. The clearing banks entered markets they had previously shunned, for example the sterling interbank market, the Finance House deposit market and the Euromarkets. Finance companies sprang up, funded by deposits from the interbank market and lending, particularly to the property market, rocketed. Unfortunately, the second aim of CCC was not fulfilled. The control of money supply growth, which had previously taken place through direct limits on lending, was now to be achieved through open market operations, i.e. by the Bank of England buying or selling bonds and bills to the market. This was unsuccessful and between 1972 and 1974 annualised money supply (M3) grew at around 24% per annum.[21]

I worked for a couple of years at a small finance company, Cripps Warburg Ltd.(CW), and saw this process at first hand. CW was able to borrow freely from the domestic and international money markets, despite a very short track record. It used this funding to build an eclectic group of businesses, including shipping finance, US investment trusts, a syndicated loan advisory department and, crucially, a UK property finance portfolio. It was this last-named department which suffered when the Government was forced to put on the monetary brakes towards the end of 1973 by calling for supplementary special deposits, thereby reverting to controlling the money supply directly. Interest rates rose steeply (to 13% in October 1973), the economy was severely affected by a huge rise in the price of oil and property values collapsed, leading to problems for companies such as CW which had lent on property.

Altogether, around 30 banks and finance companies had to be bailed out by the Bank of England, in a process which was known as the 'Lifeboat', and a further 30 had to be assisted in some way.[22] Though no depositors lost money[23], rumours swirled around the market about the financial stability of several large organisations. The largest of the 'secondary banks', those organisations which had grown rapidly during the easy money period was First National Finance Corporation (FNFC). Having rescued a smaller secondary bank – London and County – in 1974, FNFC had in its turn to be rescued by National Westminster Bank later in the year. FNFC's Chief Executive, Pat Matthews, was a larger than life character who gave rise to legends. He was reputedly driven to work daily in a chauffeured Rolls-Royce. When NatWest took over his company, they insisted on savings and said that the chauffeur-driven Rolls-Royce must go. According to the story, Pat Matthews was next seen being driven down Moorgate in a chauffeur-driven Mini.

Over Christmas 1974, the Burmah Oil Company got into difficulties and had to be bailed out by the Bank of England. Slater

Walker, a major investment firm, also needed help. These rescues were orchestrated by the Bank of England, notably by Jim Keogh, the Principal of the Bank's Discount Office, and by Rodney Galpin, Keogh's deputy. There was little analysis or criticism of the Bank's role. That was not to be the case in later bank crises.

The period from 1971 to 1973 can be read as a cautionary tale for the future. The relaxation of direct, quantitative controls on credit had liberated a huge latent demand for borrowing, both for customer and business purposes. The result was a consumer and property boom, followed by a bust. During this period, bankers came to realise that innovation was possible and also that it could be highly remunerative. Merchant banks and other financial companies sprang up like weeds. One of the largest, Slater Walker, had changed from an industrial holding company in the sixties to (in effect) an international investment bank. They were not alone. At the peak of the boom it was said that a stockbroker was busy selling the merits of shares in a laundry company. When asked what was so attractive about the laundry business, he replied, 'Not much, but the company is planning to convert itself into a merchant bank'! It is clear that some of the excesses of the early and mid–1970s presaged more recent bankers' behaviour.

Those who chose a career in banking had changed. Traditionally, the clearing banks took school leavers rather than graduates and while the situation was slightly different in the merchant banks, there were comparatively few graduates there either. Top graduates tended to go to the Civil Service (Treasury or Foreign Office), academia or multinational companies. This structure began to change in the early 1970s. The Bank of England is a case in point. 'The Bank's graduate intake doubled from 24 in 1972-3 to 48 in 1975-76.[24] Those graduates who came into the City were not always imbued with City practices and often had not taken Institute of Bankers exams. They increasingly questioned the 'way in which things were done' and were keen to adopt products from other markets, for example, financial products from the US market. While the structure of the City remained as formal and complex as ever, and bill brokers still walked the City streets with their top hats, there had been a change in behaviour, and one which was to become more pronounced with time.

For the rest of the 1970s and the first part of the 1980s, the UK economy was weak with high inflation rates. Labour problems intensified. There were no major structural changes to UK banking during this period, but banks gradually adjusted to the freer markets. This was the era of the syndicated loan, i.e. loans, usually with medium–term maturities, where there are several, sometimes many, banks lending to a borrower under a single loan agreement. Syndicated loans had been popular in the USA for many years but, as pointed out by Gadanecz, the 'first phase of [international] expansion began in the 1970s. Between 1971 and 1982, medium–term syndicated loans were widely used to channel foreign capital to the developing countries of Africa, Asia and especially Latin America.'[25] By 1982, new syndicated lending had risen to around $ 46 billion. Syndicated lending also spread to non US corporate credits. Lending came to an abrupt halt in August 1982, after Mexico suspended interest payments on its sovereign debt, soon followed by other countries including Brazil, Argentina, Venezuela and the Philippines. Lending volumes reached their lowest point at $ 9 billion in 1985. In 1987, Citibank wrote down a large proportion of its emerging market loans and several large US banks followed suit. That move catalysed the negotiation of a plan, initiated by US Treasury Secretary, Nicholas Brady,[26] which resulted in creditors exchanging their emerging market syndicated loans for Brady bonds, eponymous debt securities whose interest payments and principal benefited from varying degrees of collateralisation on US Treasuries. The Brady plan (which was, in truth, a 'smoke and mirrors' attempt to disguise the full extent of the loan impairments) provided a new impetus to the syndicated loan market which began to spread rapidly to the non–US corporate debts.

Typically, a UK company was financed by equity and bank overdraft finance. A small minority of very large companies had tapped the bond market but very few indeed had raised medium–term bank money. The development of the syndicated loan market enabled them to do so.

Syndicated loans have huge benefits. They centralise borrowing in one legal document and ensure that borrowers do not have to spend large amounts of time with many borrowers – they can spend most of the time with the lead managers and retain a more 'arms-length' relationship with the smaller participants. They enable small banks to participate in loans to the biggest companies and they provide big banks with a way of limiting their exposure to their large corporate customers. Yet they do represent a dilution of the relationship between lender and borrower. Apart from the lead manager(s), the banks and their customers would meet less frequently than if there were a 'one-to-one' relationship. In particular, if the bank had bought its participation in the secondary market (and syndicated loan participations were increasingly traded during their lifetimes) the link between the owning bank and the borrower could be very remote. Bank loans then were becoming more like bonds in that the creditor/debtor relationship was simply that: unlike the traditional banking relationship where the personal relationship between banker and borrower was an important element. The difference in practice became critical if the borrowers got into financial difficulties, as we shall see later. Of course, if the lead bank was a major lender in the banking syndicate, they might 'persuade' the rest of the syndicate to act in a traditional way, but increasingly, the lead banks saw that the best return on capital involved maximising fee income and minimising interest income, viz. taking as small a participation as possible. As a result, the lead managers often became more like investment banks than commercial banks. They were there for the fees, not the interest income and, unlike the traditional banker, they did not necessarily have a great interest in the long-term financial wellbeing of their customers.[27]

This change in banking relationships did not matter hugely when sovereign risk credits were the main form of syndicated loan. The fact that a small participant in a loan to, say, the Government of Peru, had little or no contact with Peru's Ministry of Finance was neither here nor there. They would probably have gained little by having increased contact.

Corporate loans are a different matter. It is possible to get a much better idea of a company's position by regularly meeting senior management and understanding their concerns and problems. The best of the traditional corporate bankers did this and could help their customers if times were difficult. As the syndicated loan became more common within the UK corporate market, so that traditional relationship began to dilute a little. Dennis and Mullineaux put the point as follows; 'Thus, syndicated credits lie somewhere between relationship loans and disintermediated debt.'[28]

One other change during the 1970s is worthy of note. In 1974 a German regional bank, Herstatt Bank, failed as a result of foreign exchange speculation. 'The collapse of this medium-sized bank sparked a deep crisis in the foreign exchange market, on which it was very active. The New York interbank market came to a standstill, almost leading to the collapse of a number of other institutions. This bankruptcy brought to light the systemic risks related to the increasing internationalization of banks.'[29] One consequence was that the London interbank market for US dollar deposits contracted suddenly. It was in this market that the active Eurobanks raised the finance to make their loans. Finding that the market had collapsed, many banks, particularly the Japanese banks which had become active in the syndicated loans market, found it difficult to raise money – or had to pay up (i.e. pay higher interest rates) for that money (the so-called Japanese rate). This raised the question of the liquidity of the banking system, and in particular, the liquidity of those banks which relied for their funding on borrowing from other banks in the interbank market. After this event, Peter Cooke of the Bank of England proposed the setting up of a committee, the Basel Committee, to coordinate the international regulation of banks. Basel was an important influence in establishing rules for bank capital but the other lesson of Herstatt, that liquidity can disappear if money markets contract, appeared to have been forgotten long before the 2008 banking crisis.

In domestic banking, Barclaycard's near monopoly of the credit card market had been broken by the launch of Access by

Barclays' rivals in 1972 and the introductions of widespread credit scoring had begun to break down the hegemony of the branch manager. Nevertheless, the links between banker and domestic customer remained strong. A bank manager, in a BBC interview in 1975, could say without a hint of irony that he regarded his customers as the members of a family and that he saw himself as a 'father figure' who fulfilled a similar role in the community to that of a doctor.[30]

Chapter 4

The 1980s and Big Bang

Big Bang was the single most important event to change the behaviour of banks in living memory. Before this climacteric there were a few other developments which helped make it even more radical. In November 1981, the definition of the UK banking sector was replaced '... by the wider monetary sector, consisting of all the 600 or so deposit-taking institutions recognised or licensed under the Banking Act, augmented by a number of other bodies.'[31] Also the number of eligible banks, those institutions whose accepted bills were eligible for sale to the Bank of England, was increased. The effect of both measures was to open the London market a little more. The 'Magic Circles', which had guided the City's development – and possibly also restricted its growth, were steadily breaking down.

This process was hastened by the growth in new products during the 1980s. The growth in syndicated lending has been noted. During the 1970s, the bulk of syndicated loans were for sovereign borrowers. This was thought to be a remunerative and low risk form of lending. Walt Wriston of Citibank went so far as to say that 'countries, unlike companies, do not go bust.'[32] As *The Economist* pointed out, this was patently untrue, as Citi's own history had demonstrated. Problems in Latin America had shaken the bank in 1907 and almost brought it down in 1919. Bonds issued for Peru, Bolivia and Chile in the 1920s had defaulted in the 1930s. Citibank's branches were nationalised by Russia, Egypt, China and Cuba – suggesting that even when governments are solvent, they can be toxic for banks.

His comment was seen to be either wrong or irrelevant when Mexico defaulted on its sovereign debt in August 1982, followed by a number of other (mainly) Latin American countries. But this did not spell the end of the syndicated loans market. Rather the syndicated loans market transformed itself into (principally) a source of finance for the corporate sector in the main industrialised countries, particularly the US and UK.

Many of these loans were orthodox corporate credits but there was also the arrival of the 'leveraged loan' which played an increasingly important part in the market. This product originated in the US and was, in turn, an amalgam of two types of loan, which had been active there for some time. The first was 'bootstrap finance' under which finance companies would lend to companies based on their assets. So, a company might be able to borrow say 80% of eligible debtors, 60% of work in progress and 50% of freehold property. The financier may pay some regard to the profitability of the company, but this would not be the principal consideration as long as the lender had confidence that the assets could be liquidated in the event of problems and the loans repaid. The second loan was the 'cash flow' loan under which the lender assesses the growth and certainty of the cash flow emanating from the company. As long as the lender can be confident that the company will continue to produce predictable cash flow, it may be possible for the company to borrow appreciable amounts (sometimes far larger than that justified under traditional credit analysis).

Putting these two types of finance together produced the leveraged loan under which the company geared itself up and pledged all its assets to the lending bank. The money raised could be used to distribute to shareholders (by way, for example, of share buybacks) or to fund acquisitions. Funds and other private equity companies sprang up to invest in such Leveraged Buyouts (LBOs) and to buy large companies. The largest of these private equity organisations, based in the USA, earned their senior partners huge fortunes. This was also great business for the bankers. The loans provided good interest returns– because the risks were comparatively high – and fat fees for arranging the loans and advising the various parties concerned. Banks were also sometimes involved in the ownership or management of the private equity companies who were the recipients of the leverage and, assuming the transaction was a success, earned high equity returns.

Like most new banking products, there was a good rationale for the development of the LBO. In traditional banking, all industries (more or less) were thought to be able to sustain similar levels of debt, compared to equity. The LBO attempted (at least at first) to match the level of debt to the stability and rate of growth of the company's cash flow. Such a change was of benefit to everyone as long as it did not get out of control. Soon, however, leverage increased rapidly based on hoped-for rates of growth in earnings and (sometimes wildly) optimistic estimates of the price at which assets could be sold. There were spectacular failures; the buyout of Magnet Furniture was in default soon after the deal was signed. As with so many new banking products, the bankers didn't know when to stop. Drexel Burnham, the US investment bank which pioneered the use of 'junk bonds' to finance LBO transactions, filed for bankruptcy in 1990.

It may be worthwhile pausing here to consider the change in the banker's role which the leveraged loan produced. As we have seen, the relationship between banker and corporate customer had been diluted somewhat by the emergence of the syndicated loan. The leveraged loan continued that process. As leveraged acquisitions became more common, the occasions increased where bankers to Company A were also bankers to Company B, which was trying to acquire Company A. Unsurprisingly, the management of Company A did not welcome their bankers helping a rival to buy them. In the traditional banking model, the banks chose which side to fight on. In the new world, some banks were 'common carriers of funds' whose money was available to support a commercially sensible transaction. This was a further 'chiselling away' of the relationship between banker and customer.

The leveraged loan was secured on all the assets of the company. In the event of financial difficulties, the banks tended to be less badly affected than other stakeholders – suppliers, staff and any prepaying customers. This was so under traditional secured bank lending, but in the case of the leveraged loan, the financial sector could be accused of gearing up the company in order to make a large profit, and not suffering if they got it wrong. Similar accusations would follow in future.

Another new type of product to emerge in the 1980s was the swap. In its first form, the interest rate swap, one party (A) would agree to pay the other party (B) a fixed rate of interest, say 8% p.a. on a notional amount of money, say, $ 100 million, every 6 months for a fixed period of, say, 5 years. In turn, B would pay A an amount of money linked to a particular market rate of interest, often the London Interbank Offered Rate for 6-month deposits (LIBOR). Suppose the relevant LIBOR rate was 5% p.a. for the 6-month period under consideration. At the end of the 6 months, A would be due to pay B $ 100 million times 8% divided by 2 = $ 4 million. B would be due to pay A $ 100 million times 5% divided by 2 = $ 2.5 million. In practice, A would pay B the net amount of $ 1.5 million (i.e. $ 4 million minus $ 2.5 million). Of course, if interest rates were to rise to over 8% in any period, then B would be due to pay A money. Other forms of swaps, such as currency swaps, also grew rapidly and the types of swap traded became more diverse and complex.

The great boon of swaps was that companies and banks could reduce their risks by engaging in them. A company which had borrowed on a floating rate and who wanted to know its borrowing rate long term would engage in a swap where it paid fixed and received floating. A bank who had long-term fixed rate deposits but whose loans were mainly floating rate, would engage in a swap where they received fixed rates and paid floating. Both parties would thereby benefit (assuming they wished to reduce risk).

Whilst swaps were, and still are, used for valid commercial purposes, they and other complex financial transactions such as options soon became traded assets. According to the Bank for International Settlements, the total nominal outstandings on OTC[33] derivatives contracts was around $ 630 trillion in December 2014,[34] a figure vastly larger than could be justified by commercial need alone. They have been a much greater source of profits from trading, rather than from providing customer service. Dealing for the bank's own account has rapidly outstripped customer business, so the customer became less critical to the prosperity of the 'traded assets' part of the bank. And, as traded assets themselves became an increasing contributor to bank profits, so the customer diminished in importance for the bank as a whole. (It should be noted that the transition of a 'customer market' into a 'trading market' is not unusual. The foreign exchange market is an earlier example of a similar transition.)

The implications which this had for the management of banks is dealt with by Professor John Kay in his recent book *'Other People's Money: Masters of the Universe or Servants of the People?'*[35] As Professor Kay notes in the book's website introduction,

'There is something pejorative about the phrase 'the real' – meaning the non-financial – economy, and yet it captures a genuine insight: there is something unreal about the way in which finance has evolved, dematerialised and detached itself from ordinary business and everyday life.

If buying and selling in the City not only absorbs a significant amount of our national wealth but also occupies the time of a high proportion of the ablest people in society, Humbert Wolfe's complacency – "since it contents them ... they might as well" – can no longer be easily justified. ... I shall describe how we might focus attention on a more limited finance sector, more effectively directed to real economic needs: making payments, matching borrowers with lenders, managing our money and reducing the costs of risk. We need finance. But today we have far too much of a good thing.'

With new products being developed, increasing internationalisation of banking, a more educated input into the industry and a highly sympathetic political environment, the time was perfect for Big Bang in 1986. In addition, the City, while resisting some of the changes initially, responded very positively when it became clear that the structure was going to alter.

Under Big Bang, fixed commission charges for trading stocks and shares were abolished[36] and firms for the first time could carry out both stock broking activities (acting as agents on commission) and stock jobbing (making markets in stocks and shares). Furthermore, foreigners were permitted to become members of the London Stock Exchange and trading changed from 'open outcry' to screen-based trading. The net effect of these changes was that Big Bang enabled the formation of universal banks in the UK.

The various strands of 'banking' which came together in Big Bang were in reality very different sorts of business, though they all carried the portmanteau name 'banking'. They demanded contrasting skills and, to an extent, different sorts of people.

Traditional bankers, as described by Anthony Sampson, were individuals who knew their customers well and were prepared to back their judgement by lending to them. They often combined selling and credit assessment skills (though the selling skills were not particularly advanced). They recognised that the quality of a banking portfolio could only be properly measured over the long term and, in particular, only over a period which included at least one significant downturn. For this reason, traditional lending bankers were mainly remunerated by salary (and pension) and other non-pecuniary benefits such as status, titles and grand lunches rather than by bonuses.

Even before Big Bang, lending banking had changed. The introduction of new products, such as syndicated loans, had begun to weaken the links between corporate customer and banker. And gradually bankers began to become more specialised in either sales/marketing or credit. The move away from the generalist to the specialist may have increased the professionalism of the sector to an extent but again it weakened customer/banker relationships. In many banks, credit assessment, both for companies and private individuals became more of a financial analysis and less of a judgement of the individual or corporate borrower. The improved analysis was a benefit, but the dilution of the qualitative, personal involvement was, on balance, a significant weakness.

One other change took place in the internal structure of banks which tended, against the good intentions of bank managements and regulators, to make banks riskier and also to distance bankers from their customers further. In a traditional bank, the person who dealt with the customer regularly (the branch manager in the case of personal customers and the relationship officer in the case of corporate ones) carried some, and perhaps all, of the responsibility for the credit judgement. Specialist credit departments were either small or non-existent. However, during the eighties, credit departments grew in size, professionalism and influence.

This should have been an unconditional improvement. Able, specialist credit departments, supporting relationship managers who knew their customers well, should have delivered safe decisions to the bank and financial support to their creditworthy customers. Paradoxically, it did not (and not because the credit departments were in general incompetent). What happened was that the relationship officers gradually became, in large part, salespeople and lost some responsibility for, and interest in, credit. In many cases, this happened because the salespeople were remunerated in part on revenue and saw their personal advancement in maximising income rather than generating *high quality* revenue. The customers discovered that their trusted banker had morphed into a product salesperson. This tended to happen despite the fact that in many banks the relationship officer was still 'on the hook' for the customer's credit. There was a very gradual dilution of the relationship officer's interest in credit in many banks.

Credit analysis sometimes improved but at other times the lost input from the relationship officer meant that this hoped for advantage did not happen. Things were better in those banks which allowed the credit officer access to the customer, but in many cases (especially the difficult credits) it was often in the relationship managers' interests to put obstacles in the way of the credit officer knowing the customer too well. Both in personal and corporate banking, the close ties which connected banker and customer were beginning to loosen.

As the links between the bank manager and customer weakened, so the growth in individual debt accelerated (it is not clear whether these factors were related or indeed what was the direction of causation). In 1976, UK Households' Debt to Gross Domestic Product was around 30%. Ten years later, it was over 40% and by 1990 it was approaching 60%. (It is now nearly 90%.)[37]

The traditional closed and secretive nature of the City was also beginning to alter. During the secondary banking crisis in the seventies, the Bank of England carried out its work of support lending and 'encouraged' mergers with little, if any, 'interference' or criticism from politicians or the media. The 'magic circle' was still intact. However, when Johnson Matthey failed in 1984, the Bank was criticised both for being slow in spotting the problems in a recognised bank and in failing to notify and/or get permission from the Treasury for a £ 100 million support loan. The fact that it had been accepted that no such permission was needed was irrelevant. The game had changed, and the Bank's actions henceforth would be held up to the light. Regulation had already been put on a statutory basis by the Banking Act 1979. In the 1987 Banking Act, the Bank of England was obliged to report annually to the Chancellor of the Exchequer on its supervisory activities and this report was available to Parliament. The old fashioned secretive City Club had started to break down and the Bank of England's word was no longer regarded as law.

If banking was beginning to change before Big Bang, that was nothing compared to the changes afterwards. The skills of those who arrived in the new, universal banks from stockbroking, jobbing and corporate advisory businesses were very different from those of the traditional clearing banker. Consider, for example, the skills needed by the traditional stockbroker. He (hardly ever 'she') acted purely as an intermediary between customers and/or jobbers. On occasion, the broker dealt with very large sums but took very little risk, except in the event of a bankruptcy of a counterparty or a dealing error or fraud. Yet the broker was acutely aware of those risks, however remote they may have been. Brokers firms were partnerships and the partners stood to lose personally if the firm could not pay its debts. Transported into one of the post-Big Bang universal banks, the broker was often encouraged to take 'calculated' risks with the shareholders' – i.e.

other peoples' – money. The capital available was huge. It is perhaps unsurprising that the change did not always work smoothly.

Most commentators were optimistic about Big Bang but there were some Cassandras. The *Mail Online* in 2014, reported a letter which was sent by Sir Robert Armstrong (Cabinet Secretary) to Mrs Thatcher's Private Secretary in March 1986, some 7 months before the Big Bang date of 27 October 1986. While he acknowledged his concerns were 'pretty vague and unspecific', he said that he was by no means alone in harbouring such doubts. 'I do not know whether you are having the same experience, but I am finding, among people who work outside the City of London but whose activities bring them into touch in some degree with the City, that there is increasing disquiet about the things that people think are going on in the City,' he wrote.

'I do not just mean the levels of remuneration; a lot of people, including some from inside the City, think that is a bubble that will be pricked in a year or two. They think more about the way in which corners are being cut and money is being made in ways that are at least bordering on the unscrupulous.'[38] Within a year, some of Sir Robert's qualms were borne out as the Guinness scandal erupted. This scandal involved the coordinated buying of Guinness shares so as to raise its share price and so increase the value of Guinness's bid for the Distillers Company, against competition from the Argyll Group. Four people, including Ernest Saunders, Chief Executive of Guinness, were convicted of various offences. It was closely followed by the Blue Arrow scandal where employees of County NatWest (NatWest's investment banking arm) hid the failure of a share issue which was intended to fund the takeover of Manpower Inc. by Blue Arrow. In the US there had been widespread failures in the Savings and Loans market (a sector very loosely similar to UK building societies) but these failures were thought to be irrelevant to the UK, and the Guinness and Blue Arrow affairs were regarded as isolated events. The general verdict on Big Bang was that it was a great opportunity for the City and for the UK's position within international finance.

At first it was thought that the merchant banks had the skills and sufficient capital to engage in the post-Big Bang world. After all, many of the larger merchant banks had had experience of running trading, advisory and sometimes even some banking businesses together. Big Bang should have been playing to their strengths. Most of the bigger merchant banks acquired stock brokers and/or jobbers and expanded trading, both on behalf of customers and for their own accounts. For example, SG Warburg acquired Rowe and Pitman (a stockbroker) and Akroyd (a stock jobber); Kleinwort Benson bought Grieveson Grant (broker) and Charlesworth & Co. Ltd (jobber) and Barings, notoriously, bought the broker, Henderson Crosthwaite.[39] Cultural differences existed but were managed. Reportedly one of the biggest problems in the Kleinwort/Grieveson negotiations was a dispute over lunch arrangements. The Kleinwort tradition was simple roasts carved by one of the 'home team', no wine with the meal but (remarkably) port afterwards. Grievesons favoured meals by Roux Brothers accompanied by good wine and served by gloved waiters who would remove the silver dish covers with a coordinated flourish. Grieveson's won.

Markets began to expand rapidly, and it seemed as if the merchant banks might be right. According to ISDA data, the nominal amount of derivatives outstanding rose from US$ 865.60 billion at the end of 1987 to US$ 29,035 billion a decade later[40]. The size of the Eurodollar deposit market also continued to expand. From the $ 540 billion total size in 1978 (quoted on Page 19), total Eurocurrency deposits rose to a net size of $ 1,668 billion in 1985, as estimated by Morgan Guaranty.[41]

This expansion was not costless. Kleinwort's securities dealing volume increased fourfold from 2,000 to 8,000 trades per day[42] and their back office system was not equal to the task of processing these trades until substantial investment had been made in the systems. Wags joked that there were so many contracts waiting to be processed that they had to be kept in a bike shed. Nevertheless, in the late eighties the idea that the London merchant banks could become rivals to the US investment banks was not completely far-fetched. For example, the capital resources of the largest American houses were not very different from those of the largest London merchant banks in the years leading up to Big Bang. The domination of the US equity market, which provided the fuel for the Americans' growth in power of the last three decades, did not seem, to many, to be the overwhelming influence which, in hindsight, seems so obvious. It was this, and the comparatively weak managements of many of the merchant banks which led to the eventual domination of the US houses.

While some merchant banks were acquiring securities companies and trying to become universal banks themselves, other were being absorbed into bigger organisations. For example, Morgan Grenfell was bought by Deutsche Bank in 1989. Some retail banks were also getting into the universal banking business. Barclays Bank, which had a small subsidiary called Barclays Merchant Bank (BMB), merged BMB, a stockbroker, de Zoete & Bevan and a stock jobber, Wedd Durlacher Mordaunt, to form Barclays de Zoete Wedd (BZW). NatWest, which was to become absorbed into the RBS Group in 2000, acquired a number of securities' firms to form County NatWest and Midland, HSBC bought James Capel and UBS and others all made substantial investments in the securities businesses. As pointed out by Philip Augar,[43] the European commercial banks 'suffered more than any other group of banks during the post-Big Bang period'. Having spent almost £ 500 million in buying brokers and jobbers in the 3–4 years leading up to Big Bang, these banks had to spend a similar amount in funding losses in the same period after it.

In addition, the American banks, both commercial and investment, bought into the London securities' markets. Some of them also suffered eye-watering losses (Citibank's purchase of Scrimgeour Kemp Gee is a particular case in point), but they often had the capital bases and the long-term commitment to the business to prevail.

Of the three types of institution noted above, the merchant banks were destined not to survive for long. The failure of Barings in 1995 is often given as the proximate cause of the failure of the merchant banks to compete and there is a considerable amount of truth in this. Post-Barings, funding banks understood that a failing merchant bank would not necessarily be rescued by the Bank of England and the cost of funds to the merchants immediately rose, and their profitability suffered. SG Warburg was sold to SBC, Kleinworts to Dresdner Bank and Schroders investment banking arm to Citibank. NM Rothschild remains virtually the only major UK merchant bank to be independent, based on a predominately advisory set of businesses. However, even without Barings it is unlikely, in my view, that the merchant banks would have survived. They did not possess either the size of capital or the expertise in management which were needed for the new securities-based businesses. The chairmen and chief executives of the merchant banks had traditionally come from the corporate finance advisory parts of the business, with very few from the trading areas. Whilst many (not all) of the senior directors of merchant banks were intelligent, very few had the mathematical skills to understand some of the more complex derivatives in which their banks were trading. An experienced international banker described them as 'having limited risk experience' and being 'very amateur'. Despite the huge increase in importance of the trading areas, managers from these parts of the bank, both front and back office, remained underrepresented in the ranks of senior directors. The rapid increase in trading volumes has been noted above. While some of this expansion was customer related business, a huge amount consisted of banks trading for their own account ('proprietary trades'), with the inevitable increase in risks. The ignorance of these businesses was seen in its ultimate form in the failure of Barings, following losses sustained on unauthorised trading by Nick Leeson, an options trader in their Singapore office. Not only were the Barings' senior management ill-informed about the risks involved in one of their major businesses, but they also exhibited an extraordinarily Panglossian approach to those businesses (see for example the details of Peter Baring's conversation with Brian Quinn, Director of the Bank of England in 1993, quoted below on page 55)[44]. As long as Leeson continued to make money for them,[45] the Barings management were happy.

Barings was an extreme example of a bank not knowing the nature of its new securities businesses, but other merchant banks fell for sales talk from often brilliant, plausible securities' traders. Barings was particularly unlucky to employ a crook like Leeson (and particularly stupid in having virtually no risk controls on his business) but other merchant banks lost considerable sums by investing in areas which they didn't fully understand. Merchant banks often had rigid, quite antiquated management structures which were also less flexible than their US investment banking counterparties and which sometimes appeared to be from another age. An ex-colleague of mine who went for an interview for a job in the corporate finance division, said that he felt like a gardener applying for a role at the 'Big House'.

A similar, but subtly different story was evident in those UK and commercial banks which had bought securities businesses. Philip Augar[46]elegantly describes the cultural differences in the clearing banks where the 'culture was more grammar school, more regional than Home Counties, more polyester than silk'. The 'plausible and confident' public schoolboy led merchant bankers, and brokers often persuaded their new clearing bank colleagues and 'despite their superior risk management and experience of running complex organisations, the grammar school boys at the clearing banks failed to grip the businesses they had built.'

While there is a great deal of truth in the above description there were, as Augar acknowledges, other factors at work. Clearing banking, corporate advice, asset management and securities dealing, apart from the fact that they all offer financial products, are about as different as any businesses can be. Banking is long term in character (loans can be long, and people rarely change their deposit relationships) as is asset management. Securities dealing is short term in character and advisory businesses may be either. In banking and securities dealing, the bank acts as a principal: corporate advisory and asset management are agency businesses.

Furthermore, commercial bankers need to be risk averse in the sense that they are dealing with asymmetric risks. If a loan is repaid in full and on time, the banker receives the loan principal plus interest. The profit element in this is net interest received (the interest received less interest paid to depositors). If the loan does not repay on time, the banker could lose some, and sometimes all, the principal amount, which may be many times as large as the profit element. One bad loan can erase the profits of many good ones. It is not surprising, therefore, that the traditional local clearing banker 'looked on the black side' and acquired a reputation for being very cautious. Changes in accounting practices did not help. Bankers had been used to keeping reserves 'for a rainy day' – the merchant banks, for example, had 'hidden reserves' which enabled them to squirrel away money in case it was needed. Such behaviour became more difficult as the accounting profession insisted that provisions could only be taken against current, not potential future, problems and hidden reserves were no longer permitted.

Securities trading needs different skills. Risk analysis is still vital, but the gains/losses may be more symmetrical. It may make perfect sense to take a bigger risk in order to receive a bigger expected reward, unless the capital available is insufficient to support the business in the event of problems.

It is now possible to see how 'culture wars' developed in those banks where commercial bankers had bought securities/advisory businesses. The securities traders were (understandably enough) always confident about their ability to generate profits and felt that all they needed was a bit more capital. The corporate advisors often supported them because more capital in the securities businesses meant that they could do bigger deals for their clients. The traditional bankers were frequently seen as 'stick-in-the-mud' pessimists. The banks' shareholders, keen to see sustained rapid growth, were often supporters of greater risk taking.

Most of these requests for more capital were in good faith, but it should also be noted that bigger deals and more capital were often in the personal interest of those proposing them. Traditionally, commercial bankers received higher salaries and small bonuses. On the other hand, people in the securities' businesses (and to an extent, those in the corporate advisory areas) received comparatively low salaries but high bonuses – very high in good years. It was in their personal interest to command as much capital as possible in order to trade. In the traditional stockbroking or stock jobbing firm, capital was very small and the 'animal spirits' of senior managers were controlled by the very real fear that a loss could put the future of the firm in jeopardy. The partners in the firm shared unlimited liability, so a loss for the firm was translated directly into a loss to the partners' pockets.

In the post-Big Bang world, the ex-brokers and jobbers had much more capital to play with – and no personal liability if things went wrong.

If they were successful they could earn very high bonuses and, if unsuccessful, they simply earned their basic salary (or lost their jobs, though demand for these skills was so great that even mediocre performers often found few problems in finding work elsewhere). There was no question of returning previous bonuses. This structure was an incentive to take larger risk positions. Another development reinforced this tendency. Accounting changes encouraged the taking of profits on long-term transactions in the year that the deal was done. So, for example, a 20–year swap which was calculated to produce a (discounted) profit of 100 would contribute that full 100 in year one and there might be valuation adjustments in future years. Incredibly, many bankers received their bonuses based on the year 1 profits. If the swap lost value in future years, the banker might well be working for another firm. Again, there was an encouragement of short-termism and risk taking. By the time any unfortunate consequences emerged the banker responsible might well be far away.

None of this, however, fully explains why the bonus pools were so large – in many cases large enough to eliminate most of the securities' profits even in good years. The return to (skilled) labour rose; that to capital fell markedly.

So, the commercial bankers who had bought securities and advisory businesses were confronted with a group of people who, in their opinion, were overpaid, not responsible for the long-term consequences of their actions and incapable of producing a sustained profit for the firm. The investment bankers themselves regarded their new commercial banking colleagues as out of date, boring and often a bit dim.

Unsurprisingly, cultural differences proliferated. As Philip Augar points out[47] 'At Barclays, relations between the clearing and investment bankers were described even in the BZW official history as being at "daggers drawn"'. The tensions were particularly acute in Barclays during the early and mid nineties because neither BZW nor the clearing bank seemed capable of producing a continuous growth in profits. For example, profits before tax for BZW and Barclays retail banking business were as follows, from 1990 to 1997 (when the equity business was sold to Credit Suisse First Boston): –

Profit (Loss) before tax $-\pounds$ millions

	1990	1991	1992	1993	1994	1995	1996	1997
BZW	108[48]	214[48]	241[48]	532[49]	242[49]	245[50]	190[50]	29[50]
Barclays UK Banking Services	514[48]	68[48]	(414)[48]	567[49]	1229[49]	1374[50]	1523[50]	1701[50]

Notes:

1. A substantial part of Barclays' corporate lending book was transferred into BZW in the early nineties, giving a boost to the company's profitability and providing another source of contention between the two parts of the Group.

2. Because of changes in the activities included within BZW and changes in definitions, the profit before tax figures are not strictly comparable year to year. The fact remains, however, that BZW did not present a picture of a steadily growing, healthy company.

The retail bank was on the back foot during the early part of this period, having sustained a loss in 1992 during a time when BZW appeared to be powering ahead. The BZW performance in 1993 seemed to be further evidence that investment banking was the bright future for the Group, albeit this profit was dependent in part on proprietary gains, which, in practice could not be sustained. As this became more evident and the retail banks' profits recovered while BZW's fell, so the retail bank began to exercise its power again.

I was in a particularly good position to see this unedifying argument between the two parts of Barclays as I was, for a time, employed by BZW but was also a member of the Barclays Group credit committee. Whilst people from both sides of the divide were generally polite to each other in public, there was a lot of behind the back carping. The retail banks' financial performance in the early nineties had been poor, a reflection in part of the UK domestic recession, and BZW were in the ascendant during that period, culminating in their £532 million profit in 1993 – a performance which triggered large bonus payments. During this period, BZW gradually achieved more influence in the Group and the retail bank was the butt of much criticism. However, after the 1993 *annus mirabilis,* BZW never achieved its peak performance again, while the retail bank began to recover. There was bafflement that BZW with so many bright and well-paid people could not produce a higher return. The clearing bankers appeared to get their way with the 1998 sale of BZW's equities division to CSFB (though Barclays Capital survived to enjoy renewed growth in the following decade).

While the Barclays Group was perhaps an extreme case, the development of the universal bank meant that in many places, the rivalry between clearing banker and investment banker was played out. There were, for example, stories of 'naïve' American commercial bankers paying way over the odds for UK broking firms. In one such case, the senior partner of the UK firm reportedly suggested that all the partners' wives (the partnership was wholly male) should hire the most expensive jewellery they could find for a dinner with the potential buyer. Seeing the ranks of tiaras and pearls, the American bankers concluded that the partners were so rich that a really juicy price would be needed to induce them to sell.

There were fewer 'culture wars' in those US investment banks which set up in London and grew organically. Goldman Sachs is one example of a bank which established itself in London in the seventies and grew rapidly after Big Bang. Goldmans clearly had an investment banking culture throughout.[51]

In the market as a whole, investment bankers were outright winners in that the practices of investment banking were more and more frequently introduced into commercial banking. A colleague of mine observed that it was 'mad to give [the investment bankers and traders] those huge balance sheets to trade with' and indeed the long-term effects were catastrophic for some institutions (though in the shorter term it did enable banks to expand globally more easily).

A contributory factor to the 'triumph of the investment bankers' may have been the recession of the early nineties. While there was not a particularly steep fall in GNP in that recession, some asset markets suffered very steep and protracted falls, e.g. the East Anglian property market where negative equity persisted for years. Banking profits were hit hard and, while no bank was in danger, it became common to suppose that investment banking was both more profitable and less risky than commercial banking. The universal banks put more resources into the investment banking business.

Soon there was to be a further transfer of resources which would enable even greater gambles to be taken, this time in the banking business.

Chapter 5

Demutualisation[52, 53], Liquidity and Sales

One of the less noticed aspects of financial legislation in Big Bang year (1986) was the Building Society Act. The building society sector had remained relatively unaffected by the changes which had happened in the banking sector. Building societies carried out their traditional role of lending for house purchase and accepting deposits from individuals. Most did little else, apart from some lending to and accepting deposits from other financial institutions. The regulation under which building societies operated had been 'essentially unchanged since the 1890s'.[52] The model had worked for a very long time, with very few problems, but it is important to recognise that it was not without risks. The societies were borrowing very short term, in the form of savers' deposit (and sometimes current) accounts, and lending very long term. The reason that more accidents had not occurred earlier was that the building societies knew their core business well, lending was usually well covered by security and, fortunately, really steep falls in house prices had not occurred. Furthermore, the building society sector was one where 'problem societies' were mopped up by their stronger brethren.

The Building Society Act slightly widened those activities in which the societies could engage but, equally important, it gave the societies the choice of demutualisation; i.e. the opportunity to change from an organisation owned by its members to one owned by shareholders.

Remarkably, given the rush to demutualisation later, there was little immediate interest amongst the societies. Abbey National converted into a bank in 1989, but the common view was that this was to enable Abbey to engage in a wider range of business (which they did; particularly in areas of Treasury Management).

No other society converted until 1995, when the rush began. According to the Treasury Select Committee[51], there were eight conversions between 1995 and 1999 (involving nine societies). Seven out of the largest ten societies converted and two-thirds of the sector's assets were, as a result, transferred out of the sector. Advocates of demutualisation and their opponents put forward a variety of reasons for the change, but it is difficult to escape the conclusion that the two most important influences were the ability of members to earn a capital gain ('the windfall') on conversion and the self-interest of the senior managements of many of the large societies. During the second half of the nineties, many people (the 'carpetbaggers') signed up with multiple societies in order to benefit from the expected windfall. Although this was not the effect intended by the legislation, neither the Conservative nor the Labour Governments thought it appropriate to change that legislation to prevent or discourage carpetbaggers.

The dynamics of the situation are neatly summed up by Tayler[54], 'Once the prospect of cashing in accumulated reserves was presented, it appears to have been difficult for calculating managements and generally hard up members to resist considerable immediate gain.' 'The mice were in charge of the cheese.' Big Bang swept away the restrictive practices, but also encouraged banks to think of themselves as just one type of plc.; in the business of maximising earnings per share for their shareholders. Most building societies, which had retained a social purpose well into the nineties, were swept away in the demutualisation rush and either became banks (often without the required skills) or were merged into banks.

Not all societies followed this 'primrose path'. The Nationwide Building Society is the biggest exception, but there are still 44[55] mutual societies extant, albeit mainly very small, local societies. Most survived by modifying '… their rules of membership in the late 1990s. The methods usually adopted were membership rules to ensure that anyone newly joining a society would, for the first few years, be unable to get any profit out of a demutu-alisation. With the chance of a quick profit removed, the wave of demutualisations came to an end in 2000.'[56] The true reason for demutualisation was thereby revealed.

The demutualisation story illustrates just how far the finan-cial services industries had come since the ordered days of the post-war period. There were some voices arguing that members of building societies were, in effect, trustees for money built up by past generations to benefit this and future ones. This argu-ment was rejected as a matter of law but, more important, many people rejected the whole concept. There was a widespread view that carpet-bagging was a perfectly acceptable, indeed desirable, practice. If there was a free lunch going, why not accept it? Even though the resources of building societies had never intended to be distributed amongst a lucky generation, this was regarded as fair game. The managements, as Tayler points out, often led the charge towards demutualisation, realising that they would gain the most.

Many of those who criticised the banks in the 2008 crash must have been carpetbaggers a decade earlier. They were sub-ject to the same greed which affected the 'bonus' bankers, ex-cept for the fact that the amounts were so much smaller and for the fact that the carpetbaggers had done absolutely nothing to justify their windfalls.

It is instructive to follow what happened to the demutualised building societies. The theory, it should be remembered, was that they would be able to compete with the banks for business, staff, and deposits and would become more efficient as a result. As pointed out by Ian Pollock, on the BBC News Channel on 29 September 2008[57], some felt that 'What looked like a good way of expanding business and becoming a modern, thrusting … or-ganisation … became … a new and exciting way to lose money'. The managements of the newly minted banks forgot that they were running risky structures and became increasingly involved in more complex and riskier products. Some organisations be-gan to lend more than 100 % of the property's value. Some pros-pered in the short term but [most] encountered difficulties. By late 2008, all the demutualised building societies had either been absorbed into other banks (one at least of which had in turn to be rescued) or nationalised. No one (to my knowledge) has estimated the cost to the taxpayer which has resulted from demutualisation. Such an exercise would be very complex, and the underlying assumptions would be subject to considerable debate. Nevertheless, it may be worth doing in order to forestall any similarly cavalier pieces of legislation in future.

By the second half of the nineties, complex, risk management tools had permeated the banking sector. Loans were there to be bought and sold, securitised, sliced and diced and not held to maturity. And while there were still many bankers who diligently tried to help their customers and clients, the banks themselves gave a fair impression that they were much more concerned with the financial performance of their portfolio than the wellbeing of their customers. This was so both at the retail and wholesale end of the banking spectrum. Retail banks were steadily closing branches and the figure of a known 'bank manager' was becoming less common. The number of bank branches in the UK, which began to fall in the eighties and nineties, continued its decline. The number is now around 8,000[58], compared with just over double that number (16,132) in 1989.[59]

The US Congress repealed the Glass–Steagall Act in November 1999. As observed by Joseph E Stiglitz[60], 'the most important consequence of the repeal of Glass–Steagall was indirect – it lay in the way repeal changed an entire culture. Commercial banks are not supposed to be high-risk ventures ... It is with this understanding that the government agrees to pick up the tab should they fail. Investment banks, on the other hand, have traditionally managed rich people's money – people who can take bigger risks to get bigger returns. When repeal of Glass–Steagall brought investment and commercial banks together, the investment bank culture came out on top.' In the UK there was a similar cultural takeover, which began earlier with Big Bang and was reinforced by the demutualisation of the building societies. As I point out earlier, it appeared in the early 1990s that commercial banking was inherently less profitable and more risky than investment banking. The trading mentality permeated the banks and traders gradually attained greater power within the organisations, leading eventually to the appointment of, for example, Bob Diamond as CEO of Barclays.

I have mentioned that the relationship between banker and corporate customer suffered as a result of the development of banking products such as syndicated loans and securitisation and the movement towards more transactional banking. The close relationship which used to pertain was diluted. If the bank had sold all their loans to others it was difficult to preserve the banker–customer relationship. No longer could the customer be confident that the banker was giving advice which was even handed and unbiased. The situation became even worse as more sophisticated products were developed. The growth of short selling meant that your helpful bank might have a vested interest in your company doing badly. I was the Chairman of a couple of public companies between 2000 and 2011 and there were times that I suspected that some of our advising banks had very different aims and objectives from ourselves. We were much less valued customers than the hedge funds and other investors who were taking both long and short positions in our shares. That is not to say that the 'trusted advisor' entirely disappeared from the banking scene. I and my colleagues were lucky enough to benefit from some really top quality, and ethically strong, advisors. However, this species, if not endangered, became rarer during the nineties and the early years of the new century. Despite strict 'conflict of interest' rules, it became commonplace to wonder why the investment banking advisor was giving a particular piece of advice: What was their angle? Did they have other, more important, customers who would benefit from the advice given? Or perhaps the investment bank itself had a position and would gain if the advice was taken.

Where a bank makes a loan to a customer and keeps it to maturity, the interests of the bank and customer are aligned; they both have an interest in the wellbeingof the customer. When the bank has sold the loan or, worse, is short of the customer's shares, there is no longer an identity of interests.

Chapter 6

Light touch Regulation 1997–2008

Two of the early acts of the new Labour Government in 1997 were to grant the Bank of England the freedom to set interest rates without the need to consult government and to transfer the responsibility for bank regulation away from the Bank to the newly formed Financial Services Authority (FSA).

Part of the reason for the setting up of the FSA was undoubtedly the wish not to concentrate too much power in the Bank's hands. But there was also a feeling that the 'old style' bank supervision, which characterised the Bank of England's approach, had been found wanting. During the previous 10 years there had been two bank failures, Bank of Credit and Commerce International (BCCI) and Barings. In the case of BCCI there had been a report, produced in 1992 by 'Sir Thomas Bingham, at that time a Lord Justice of Appeal, [which was] littered with criticisms of the Bank'[61], but no changes in the structure of supervision were recommended. Bingham felt that the Bank had been lacking in alertness but that the underlying system was sound.

In the Baring's case, the Treasury Committee was much more critical. 'Given that the controls within Barings have subsequently been exposed as woefully inadequate, this must raise critical questions over the way the Bank performs its supervision and the way it evaluates the banks for which it is responsible.'[62] There was a view that a more systematic and quantitative approach to regulation was necessary. The (admittedly caricatured) view of the Bank of England's approach to regulation was that it depended too much on getting to know bank managements over lunch and too little on understanding the new types of business, such as derivatives trading, in which the banks were engaging.

Whilst there may have been some truth in this caricature, it was misleading in two respects. First, the Bank of England seemed to come under more criticism for its actions (or lack of them) over Barings than over BCCI. Yet, no retail depositor or investor lost money in the Barings crash, while they did so in BCCI. In terms of outcomes, BCCI was a crash where the regulators perhaps should have intervened. I'm not sure that there was any need for the regulator to involve itself in a medium sized merchant bank whose failure had little systemic importance and where the general public lost no money.

There was, however, a serious lesson to be learnt from the Barings collapse. It was that both regulators and managements should understand in detail the businesses for which they were responsible. In a notorious comment to Brian Quinn, Director of the Bank of England when things looked to be going well, Peter Baring, Chairman of Barings said:

'The recovery in profitability has been amazing following the [1993] reorganisation, leaving Barings to conclude that it was not actually terribly difficult to make money in the securities markets'.[63]

If ever there was a comment which summarised the lack of understanding of the new businesses by the old-style bankers, this was it. Unfortunately, this lesson was not taken to heart. This sentiment was shared by many other bankers over the following decade, with catastrophic results. Furthermore, many of the traders themselves did not fully understand the products they were trading and, in particular, assumed that markets would continue to be benign indefinitely.

Secondly, and perhaps more tellingly, the new regulatory structure was much less effective than its predecessor. One of the reasons for this was that there were three organisations involved in trying to avoid widespread bank failure. The FSA had the responsibility for individual bank supervision, the Bank of England retained the responsibility for monitoring 'financial stability' and HM Treasury had overall responsibility for the running of economic policy. The various responsibilities were outlined in a 'Memorandum of Understanding'.

Although the Bank of England kept a responsibility for financial stability, there appears to have been insufficient exchange of information between the Bank and the FSA on the state of individual banks. The Bank did some work on systemic risk and other threats to the banking system but gradually the organisation became more focused on interest rate policy and the financial stability side of the organisation received fewer resources. Under Mervyn King's governorship that trend accelerated. The new governor, unlike Eddie George, did not enjoy meeting bankers very much and many of the bankers could not see the point in meeting the Bank of England. Their regulatory 'bosses' were, after all, the FSA. How could the Bank of England help – or harm – them? Thus, the Bank of England gradually lost touch with senior bankers and institutionally became less adept at judging whether those senior managers were a threat to, or a bulwark in, support of stability. It would be wrong to say that all contact broke down. Alastair Clark and Paul Tucker (two executive directors of the Bank) attempted to keep contacts going. But it was an uphill task. Thus, the Bank of England, who had the responsibility for financial stability, neither had access to the data on individual banks, nor a detailed knowledge of the behaviour and character of the people running those banks. The work which tended to get done on financial stability was 'top down' academic work which, while useful, was not enough to help manage a banking system which was becoming dangerously adventuresome.

For its part, the FSA concentrated on individual bank supervision and really didn't do much on financial stability. Understandably, they thought of this as primarily the job of the Bank of England. The Treasury did not appear to notice that a significant element of control over the banking system was not being carried out. As Gordon Brown admitted in 2011:

'We know in retrospect what we missed. ... [W]e created a monitoring system which was looking at individual institutions.

That was the big mistake. We didn't understand how risks were spread across the system, we didn't understand the entanglements of different institutions with the other and we didn't understand ... just how global things were ...'[64]

Brown observed that 'just about everybody' in the regulatory business made the same mistake. While that observation was probably true, we should pause for a moment to consider how extraordinary a comment it is. Virtually nobody in an industry paid for by the taxpayer and charged with the job of keeping the banks under control, recognised that the fates of the banks were interconnected.

The case for the view that banks should be allowed to pursue their business without undue interference was made eloquently by Oliver Lodge in 'A Review of the UK Banking Industry'.[65] In the introduction to that report, Howard Flight[66] notes that the industry had felt 'bombarded' by 18 government inquiries and 'interventions' between 1997 and 2002. Clearly there was no shortage of government interest in how the banks should be controlled. Yet the prevailing view, both on the left and the right, was that 'light touch regulation' was the appropriate way to encourage competition and innovation in the banking industry. The possibility of systemic risk was not mentioned in the overview of the Lodge Report.

That report was published by the Centre for Policy Studies, a free market group set up by Sir Keith Joseph. A bias against regulation might, therefore, be expected. But, as noted above, the principles of light regulation and self-regulation for banks became the conventional wisdom across most of the political spectrum.

The following excerpt from a London University paper by Philip Rawlins and others, captures the point:

Blair saw the FSA's approach as indicative of a general tendency to over-regulate: 'The result is a plethora of rules, guidelines, responses to 'scandals' of one nature or another that ends up having utterly perverse consequences.' He added: 'Something is seriously awry ... when the Financial Services Authority that was established to provide clear guidelines and rules for the financial services sector and to protect the consumer against the fraudulent, is seen as hugely inhibiting of efficient business by perfectly respectable companies that have never defrauded anyone; when pensions protection inflates dramatically the cost of selling pensions to middle income people ...'[67]

The Blair and Brown governments did concern themselves with the banking sector but many of the interventions and reports focussed on the lack of competition in the UK banking system, not on its inherent instability. See, for example, Don Cruickshank's highly critical report and *The Telegraph's* comments on the lack of follow-up.

'It is 12 months since Don Cruickshank published his damning report on the banking sector, in which he accused the high street banks of overcharging customers, anti-competitive practices and creating confusion about the fees and conditions attached to various products.'[68] *The Telegraph* observed that, despite the welcome, the report received from the government, the FSA and the Consumers' Association, very little was done to address the shortcomings which the Cruickshank report highlighted.

The Hampton Report[69] looked at increasing the efficiency of regulation in a number of different spheres; the implicit assumption being that, if anything, there was too much control over the 'animal spirits' of bankers and other business people.

Despite the pressure for less regulation, an event occurred in the USA in 1998 which should have given cause for concern. Long Term Capital Management (LTCM) was a hedge fund, set up in 1993 by the ex-Solomon Brothers' trader, John Meriwether, and involving both bond traders and academic economists in its management. Amongst the economists were Myron S Scholes and Robert C Merton who jointly won the Nobel Prize in 1997 for their work on options. The fund produced very high returns from inception to 1997, based on arbitrage between different bonds and derivatives and bond and derivatives markets. Because the price differences between these different instruments were very small, LTCM had to borrow huge amounts of money compared with its capital in order to produce a high return on that capital.

Unfortunately, that meant that any loss would also be magnified hugely. And in 1998, LTCM failed to predict the Russian default on domestic bonds and had to be rescued by a consortium of 15 banks, 'encouraged' by the Federal Reserve Bank of New York.[70]

The lessons which could have been learned from this episode included:

» Complicated derivative-based businesses are dangerous and can lead to outcomes unforeseen by even the cleverest of practitioners.

» Rescuing organisations which would otherwise fail can lead to 'moral hazard'; that is to say, organisations may be prone to take high risks because if they succeed they will make lots of money, but if they fail they will be rescued. Either way, the organisation does not suffer the full cost of the high risks taken and there is an incentive to take imprudent business decisions.[71]

» Where a failure threatens the global banking system, more rather than less regulation is necessary. That LTCM was such a threat is evident from the following extract from an International Monetary Fund survey, published in 1998:

'… With the benefit of hindsight, it is safe to conclude that the outright failure of LTCM would have posed significant risks of systemic problems in international financial markets, and that it was necessary to restructure LTCM. A more rapid and disorderly unwinding of LTCM's very large and highly leveraged fixed-income positions and related positions of other institutions could have triggered an even more destructive forced deleveraging in US, German, and Japanese fixed-income markets and in the major currency markets. This would have necessarily included equally disruptive selling pressures in the associated derivative markets, where the volume and notional value of transactions are several multiples of the volume and face value of the underlying securities. One can only speculate how much worse the market turbulence would have been had LTCM been allowed to collapse.'[72]

None of these lessons were learnt and, in particular, regulation steadily became more relaxed For example, according to Joseph E Stiglitz, Larry Summers' 'great achievement' as Deputy Secretary of the Treasury, from 1999 to 2001, was passage of the law that ensured that derivatives would not be regulated – a decision that helped blow up the financial markets.'[73] For example, on 30 July 1998, then-Deputy Secretary of the Treasury, Summers, testified before the US Congress that 'the parties to these kinds of contract are largely sophisticated financial institutions that would appear to be eminently capable of protecting themselves from fraud and counterparty insolvencies.' At the time, Summers stated that 'to date, there has been no clear evidence of a need for additional regulation of the institutional OTC derivatives market, and we would submit that proponents of such regulation must bear the burden of demonstrating that need.'[74]

Perhaps the clearest example of the 'hands off' approach by the regulators was the Basle 2 rules. The Basle accords were instituted in 1988 in the wake of the Herstatt Bank collapse (see page 28) in a laudable attempt to set up consistent minimum capital requirement for banks throughout the world. In that, they have met with considerable success. However, Basle 1 was a blunt instrument in that there was little distinction between the capital required to support loan portfolios with very different risk characteristics. Whether the bank was lending to major international corporations or highly borrowed management buyouts, the capital required was the same. Basle 2 was published initially in 2004 and was intended to be risk sensitive, in that more capital would be required for more risky portfolios. Capital was to be fixed at a level which should be sufficient (on certain risk assumptions) for the bank to survive for 999 out of every 1000 years. So far so good. What was remarkable about Basle 2 was that the big banks were allowed to construct their own models of risk against which their capital was judged. Unsurprisingly, it was in the interests of the bankers – and often in their immediate and considerable individual pecuniary advantage – to minimise those capital requirements. They had more 'skin in the game' and often succeeded in arguing for lower capital ratios, based on supposedly lower risk profiles. The moves towards more professional risk management; better governance and improved transparency, which were meant to attend the freedom of banks to produce their own risk models, just didn't happen. The extent of the leveraging of UK banks in the early years of the new Millennium can be seen from the graph below, taken from a paper by Professor David Miles.

Figure 1. UK Banks leverage and real GDP growth (10-year moving average)[75]

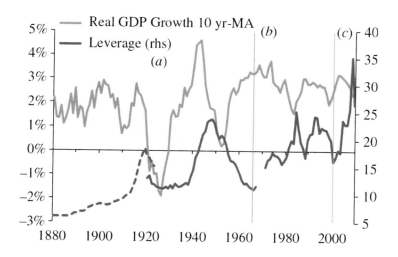

The figures used here are for overall leveraging and do not take into account changes in the risk profile, but they show a quite remarkable increase in bank debt. Between 1980 and 2000, UK banks' leveraging averaged around 20 times (i.e. capital and reserves represented around 5 % of the balance sheets). The figure was quite volatile and a considerable increase on the 15 times leverage in the sixties and seventies. But it was nothing compared with the leverage between 2000 and 2007, which shot up to 35 times at the maximum. At these levels, equity and reserves were less than 3% of the balance sheets and, as we now know, many of the assets were highly risky.

The question then arises, 'How did the regulators and the banks themselves fool themselves into thinking that these levels of leverage were compatible with a "once in a thousand years" default event?' I do not think that there were many deliberate attempts by bankers to mislead the regulators because it appears that the bankers themselves were generally convinced by their own arguments. Within the context of a belief in the effectiveness of market forces in driving discipline, several factors contributed to that unjustified complacency:

» Many of the banking products had only been in existence for a short period of time. To extrapolate that they were safe over a 1000-year period involved assumptions about the external environment which were rarely made explicit. In many cases, neither the senior managers of the banks nor their traders fully understood these assumptions.

» It was often assumed that risk events were independent: that the chance of a default in one portfolio did not influence or was not influenced by the chance of a default in another portfolio. This assumption was shown to be at fault in 2008. Events influenced many portfolios at the same time. If bankers had paid more attention to adages such as, 'It never rains but it pours' rather than assumptions of statistical independence, perhaps leverage would have been kept under control.

» A huge amount of reliance was placed on rating agencies' assessment of creditworthiness. Before issuing a new transaction, banks would 'shop around' amongst the rating agencies to see who would provide the strongest rating. The agencies were paid by the issuers, so it was not in their interest to provide too conservative a rating.[76] The portrayal of the incompetent and venal Ratings Agency executive in the film *The Big Short* may not have been too wide of the mark.

» Often, the new products traded by the banks were mathematically complex. Banks employed able mathematicians to design and to control these areas but their boards (and often senior managements) did not fully understand them and the mathematicians themselves had not experienced a serious downturn. Very few people had the range of skills and experience necessary to handle these dangerous products. There was a view that the bankers knew what they were doing, and no new regulation was required to control these 'beasts'. As quoted on page 60, on 30 July 1998, Deputy Secretary of the Treasury, Summers, testified before the US Congress that 'the parties to these kinds of contract are largely sophisticated financial institutions that would appear to be eminently capable of protecting themselves from fraud and counterparty insolvencies.' At the time, Summers stated that 'to date there has been no clear evidence of a need for additional regulation of the institutional OTC derivatives market, and we would submit that proponents of such regulation must bear the burden of demonstrating that need.'[77] A few years later, Summers was provided with more than sufficient evidence.

» Whilst those instruments were mathematically complex, the assumptions about their likelihood of default were often extremely simple and, as it turned out, naïve. Robert C Merton who was a Director of Long Term Capital Management (LTCM) and who was awarded the 1997 Nobel Memorial Prize for Economics, gave a talk to Vassar College in 1998. I am told that in the talk he said that, in order for LTCM to be insolvent, a 'one in ten thousand years' event would have to take place. Within a short time, two such events happened and LTCM had to be rescued.

» Bank managements often put an absurd amount of reliance on simple measures of risk such as Value at Risk (VAR). Some even believed that the VAR measure indicated the maximum loss that could be sustained on an investment, rather than a sum which (based on certain assumptions) was likely not to be exceeded in a certain percentage of occurrences. Yet other managements were more canny. I had a boss (not a mathematician) who would ask the question, 'What are the chances of the VAR figure being exceeded between now and the date I retire?' This line of enquiry would not have prevented the LTCM type of error but successfully avoided some of the traps in this type of business. In general, there was far too much trust in mathematical algorithms and far too little 'common sense' questioning of these complex and difficult products.

Banks not only made do with much lower levels of capital than hitherto, but they also increasingly used a method called securitisation in order to do increasing amounts of business with the same capital base. Essentially, securitisation worked as follows. A bank would set up a special purpose company (SPV) to buy, say, some loans from the bank's portfolio. The SPV would fund itself with loans from other banks (senior loans) and with various levels of subordinated debt and equity provided by the bank and other financial institutions. The trick was to arrange a capital structure in the SPV (and/or security structures), which ensured that the senior loans were very highly rated by the ratings agency (usually AAA) and, therefore, that the banks making the senior loans had to hold very low levels of capital against these loans. The net result was that the financial community had, in aggregate, to hold less capital against a group of loans that were securitised than against those loans when they were on the banks' balance sheets.[78] That was so even though the underlying risk had not changed. Very few bankers – and this is the truly extraordinary part – appeared to question why the simple act of restructuring should have produced so much reduction in the amount of regulatory capital required. It is worth noting again that it was usually in the bankers' short term pecuniary interest to minimise capital.

We have described the banks' and regulators' approach to capital. There was an equally lax attitude towards the amount of liquidity banks should hold.

Liquidity is central to a bank's existence. Banks are unusual organisations in that they 'borrow short and lend long': in the technical jargon they 'transform maturities'. No bank could ever pay out every penny of customer deposits, if all depositors tried to withdraw their deposits at the same time. Banks should keep enough assets in liquid (easily sellable) form, such that any reasonable request to withdraw funds can be satisfied. They should be wary of high concentrations of very long-term assets which can't be easily converted into cash and of reliance on volatile deposit sources.

We outlined above the reduction in capital which has occurred during the post-war period. The same happened to liquidity. In 1968,[79] the average UK bank held 20.5% of its deposits in liquid form, i.e. in deposits at the Bank of England or in cash. By 1998, that ratio had fallen to 3.1%. This fall probably underestimates the true decline in liquidity because, during this time, bank products had become much more complex and also banks had begun lending for much longer periods, sometimes up to 25 years' maturity[80]. Those arguing for lower liquidity ratios would no doubt point to the fact that bank loans and other assets had become much more tradeable. Which is true, except that when the crash came, these supposedly marketable assets often proved difficult, if not impossible, to sell.

Northern Rock, the building society which became a bank in 1997, operated on the basis of funding a very long-term mortgage book with short-term deposits raised in the money markets (i.e. by borrowing short term from other banks) and through securitisation. Despite a scare in 2004 when interest rates rose and Northern Rock '... promised investors that half its loans would be matched by retail deposits', the bank continued to be reliant on wholesale sources of funding and when funding problems surfaced in 2007, three quarters of Northern Rock's sources of funding was wholesale in nature. The beginnings of the 'freezing' of the securitisation market early in 2007 and the collapse of the money market later in the year meant that Northern Rock lost an appreciable portion of its funding very quickly. Rapidly, a run on the bank developed – the first such run on a UK bank in 140 years – and the bank had to be rescued. As *The Economist* noted, [81]'Adam Applegarth, the mortgage bank's chief executive, and Matt Ridley, its chairman, tried to convince a sceptical parliamentary committee investigating the fiasco that they had been struck down by a bolt from the blue.' It may be worthwhile pausing to see whether Northern Rock was truly unlucky or whether their problems could have been foreseen.

The interbank deposit and securitisation markets, on which Northern Rock relied so heavily, had been liquid and deep for many years. Yet there had been a period in the 1970s when the interbank market had stalled following the Herstatt crisis (see page 28). Was it prudent for Northern Rock to bet the whole bank on these markets remaining healthy? At the very least, Northern Rock should have noticed that their funding policy was different, and more risky than those of their competitors and taken action accordingly. Their difficulties were not a 'bolt from the blue'.

The fact that a bank cannot pay its debts when due does not necessarily mean that its assets are worth less than its liabilities. The bank may be suffering from a pure liquidity problem. In the seventies, there was a run on a major international bank on one of the outer islands in Hong Kong and the branch actually ran out of cash. The situation was quickly remedied by cash sent in a speedboat from the main Hong Kong office. More frequently of course, liquidity problems arise because there are doubts over the quality of the bank's assets. Customers who are concerned about asset quality withdraw their funds and this precipitates a liquidity problem.

The situation in 2007/8 was that some banks faced the predicament that their assets were beginning to be questioned and they had very little capital or liquidity with which to answer these questions. It is not surprising that Royal Bank of Scotland and Lloyds, which had involved themselves in foolhardy acquisitions, were the most badly affected. Nor was it surprising, given the *laissez-faire* regime, that the regulators did not appear to notice what was happening. The attitude of the regulators can be summed up by this *mea culpa* which appeared in the FSA's report on the failure of the Royal Bank of Scotland Group.[82]

'... many aspects of the FSA's approach to the supervision of systemically important firms in the pre-crisis period were inadequate. This reflected the fact that the FSA's overall philosophy and approach was flawed. There was insufficient focus on the core prudential issues of capital and liquidity, and inadequate attention given to key business risks and asset quality issues. Too much reliance was placed on assessments that appropriate decision-making processes were in place, with insufficient challenge to management assumptions and judgements. And a flawed concept of a 'regulatory dividend' rewarded firms with less intensive supervision if they could demonstrate effective controls and displayed a degree of cooperation with the FSA that ought to have been a non-negotiable minimum. Reflecting this philosophy, insufficient resources were devoted to high impact banks and in particular to their investment banking activities.'

Such a view calls into question Gordon Brown's observation (which we noted on page 56) that the mistake had been to look at individual bank creditworthiness and ignore systemic problems.

'We know in retrospect what we missed. We set up the Financial Services Authority (FSA) believing that the problem would come from the failure of an individual institution,' he said. 'So, we created a monitoring system which was looking at individual institutions. That was the big mistake. We didn't understand how risk was spread across the system, we didn't understand the entanglements of different institutions with the other and we didn't understand, even though we talked about it, just how global things were, including a shadow banking system as well as a banking system. That was our mistake, but I'm afraid it was a mistake made by just about everybody who was in the regulatory business.'[83]

The truth was different. Not only was the regulatory system not set up to look at systemic risk (to that extent, Brown was correct) but, as the FSA itself admitted, its regulation of individual banks was also inadequate.

What is surprising is that supposedly professional boards and managements got themselves into this pickle. The following chapter tries to assess why this occurred.

Chapter 7

Who's in Charge?

In theory there are at least five groups able to intervene to help prevent banks taking really poor decisions – or at least to point out that such decisions are being taken. These are management, the board of directors, shareholders, regulators and rating agencies. We have seen above how the regulatory structure failed in the years leading up to 2008. This chapter will attempt to show how the other 'fail safe' controls were inadequate.

Fifty years ago, banking was a recognised profession. Many operating bankers were members of the Institute of Bankers and the job of a banker was in principle a well-defined one. It was not a simple business, but it was one which was capable of being managed. Cartels and other constraints on trade often made the job easier for managements and operating bankers alike. If, for example, fees were fixed for a certain type of business, that removed one major source of uncertainty.

The enormous expansion in the number, diversity and complexity of banking products over the last few decades and the formation of vast and complicated universal banks made some of the approaches of the traditional banker outdated (though some – such as an awareness of liquidity – were forgotten which perhaps ought to have been retained). Fundamental to this approach was the view that banks were, in essence, little different from any other private sector limited companies. They were there to maximise (long term) profits without caring too much about their social role.

Along with the view that banks were like any other commercial organisation, came the idea that you didn't really need a banker to run a bank – a good businessperson would do. So, Fred Goodwin, having worked as an accountant at Touche Ross, joined National Australia Bank in 1995 as Deputy Chief Executive before moving to RBS in 1998 as Deputy CEO and, later, CEO. He was chosen by the board, led by George Mathewson, RBS's Chairman[84], who had been spectacularly successful in growing the bank but who, interestingly, also had 'relatively little banking experience'[85]. Andy Hornby had a stellar career in Asda before being appointed as Halifax Chief Executive in 1999 and as CEO of HBOS in 2001 following the merger with Bank of Scotland.

Part of the logic was that banks no longer did what banks used to do. In 1980, non-interest income for major UK banks amounted to under 30% of interest income[86]; by 2005, this ratio had increased to 180% and though there was a precipitate fall to 40% in 2007–8, the ratio has since then climbed back up to the 180% level again. Clearly the business of taking in deposits and lending them out no longer forms the majority of a bank's business. Furthermore, as we saw earlier, the front-line bankers had shuffled off the credit function into a specialist area, rather than regarding credit as a core competence of every banker. In the new bank structures, many of the senior 'front office' positions did not appear to demand traditional banking skills. Why then employ traditional bankers – can't others skilled in sales and marketing do a better job?

The reason, I believe that we still need traditional banking skills throughout the banks, is that risk performs a role in banking which it doesn't in most other sectors (excluding some others such as insurance). Risk for a banker is, in effect, the product. Whether it is an intraday trading risk or a long-term illiquid loan, the banker's role is to run a portfolio of those risks in a way which retains the confidence of the depositors.

» This point is highlighted by the following quotations from Professor Julian Franks and Dr Peter Hahn in their submissions to the Parliamentary Commission on Banking Standards:[87]

What is different about banks is that they give rise to tremendous systemic risks. Whereas BP can destroy itself but the taxpayer does not bail the company out, it is the preponderance of leverage and the failure that gives rise to systemic risk that make banks different. (Professor Julian Franks)[88]

Banks, however, are fundamentally risk management businesses; their business is to try to match risk and return on a daily basis. [...] the challenge is that it is very hard for many large businesses to change their risk profile very quickly, and a bank could take on unbelievable amounts of risk in a few moments. (Dr Peter Hahn)[89]

Instead of the idea of banker as risk manager, many bankers believed their job was to generate lots of assets and profits, keep the confidence of the shareholders and leave it to the risk department to maintain control. Johnny Cameron of RBS said in 2013, 'With hindsight, dreadful things happened because the risk managers didn't spot the wrongdoing.[90] There seemed to be little recognition that the control of risk is a, perhaps *the*, paramount senior management responsibility. Contrast Cameron's statement with the behaviour of another – earlier – incomer into banking management, Martin Taylor at Barclays, who made sure that he understood the risks that were being taken by, for example, taking a role in chairing Barclays' Credit Committee. Bank managements may have been remiss in ignoring or miscalculating risks, but they were trying to run organisations of hideous complexity. Furthermore, management training in banks was generally not up to the level in the best non-financial companies, while the management challenge they faced was one of the most difficult.

As I mention earlier, neither those running the banks nor the traders themselves often thoroughly understood the risk characteristics of the products that the bank was trading.

If the managers of the banks were not capable of, or interested in, controlling the tigers they had by the tail, it is perhaps being overoptimistic to think that the boards could do so. As the Parliamentary Commission on Banking Standards noted, 'The complexity of banks led some witnesses to express scepticism that it was possible for a bank board to work as effectively as was the case in other sectors. This was the Governor's stance: certain "institutions were simply too big and complex for anyone to genuinely know exactly what was going on."'[91]

The problem in essence was that there were very few people who knew enough about those parts of the bank which could bust the organisation and even fewer were independent. There is still little consensus about the extent to which 'non-executive' directors (NEDs) should be involved in the actual running of the banks. The current view is that they should be more closely involved, particularly in the areas of risk management and the 'senior managers' regime', introduced by the regulators last year (2017) reflects that view. However, an inevitable consequence of this is that the NEDs will become more a part of the decision-making process and their independence may thereby be compromised.

What is clear is that in the run up to 2008, boards of directors did little or nothing to curb the exuberance of their management teams. Given the complexity of the banks, this was perhaps unsurprising. As Professor Julian Franks put it in his evidence to the Parliamentary Committee on Banking Standards[92,] 'banks are very complex organizations and increasingly I am coming to the view that bank boards do not have the information to pinpoint problems early enough. Problems of fraud, mis-selling as well as excessive leverage should tell us that with the best of directors some banks are simply too complex for boards to manage with confidence.'

Yet, if the banks were so complex, why did so many experienced and bright people elect to join bank boards? Was it the kudos, the money or a kind of inertia which assumed that these were organisations which were so much part of the establishment that they could not fail. I believe that these factors did play a part but that there was also a touching faith in the form of governance. As long as the bank had the approved structures (and, for example, RBS had a highly regarded governance structure) this was regarded as 'job done' by the board. If the board had looked more closely beneath the surface and tried to judge the increasingly eccentric regime which Fred Goodwin was running, they may have taken action earlier. I am not saying that such judgements are always easy. Fred Goodwin was a highly respected and successful CEO and to have challenged him would have been extremely difficult. But that is precisely what boards are there to do. And it was not as if there were no warning signs. The FSA's report on RBS concluded, according to *The Guardian*, that the FSA had serious concerns about RBS as early as 2003. 'A year later, officials within the regulator became so concerned about Goodwin's dominance that they considered sending in a team of independent scrutineers to review how the bank was run. The action was not taken after lobbying from RBS non-executive directors, who insisted they could keep Goodwin's dictatorial impulses in check. Former directors and other senior staff have latterly claimed Goodwin had been "bullying". Morning meeting conference calls between executives were known by some as the "morning beatings".'[93] If the board of directors did have any serious reservations about Goodwin, they were, nevertheless, prepared to defend him against the regulator and, perhaps more important, did not seem to be prepared to confront him with these concerns.

It is worthwhile also to remember that, in most cases, the boards of directors who presided over the collapse of RBS and HBOS (and who received direct support from government sources totalling £ 532 billion at its peak) have gone on to lucrative board memberships elsewhere.[94] Patrick Hoskins in *The Times*[95] describes the careers of some of the 'Lloyds fifteen' who have gone on to other board appointments, without apparently suffering from their association with the Lloyds debacle.

The third line of defence is meant to be the shareholders, who can keep an eye on errant managements and banks.

Most UK banks are plc's and were so at the beginning of the Millennium. They answer to shareholders who are overwhelmingly institutional in character. Furthermore, there has been a significant decline in the proportion of UK banks' shares held by UK institutions and a rise in the proportion held by overseas institutions.[96] Most portfolio managers at these institutions (UK and overseas) are paid accordingly to their short-term (quarterly or annual) performance so, perhaps understandingly enough, most of their interaction with their investee companies is to encourage them to increase short-term Earnings per Share. (There were and are some notable exceptions to this observation – institutional investors who are prepared to take long-term views based on their judgement of managements and businesses – but they are a minority.) There is little evidence that the shareholders attempt to control risk taking in the banks (even if the institutions had the information to judge those risks) because they have every incentive to encourage risk-taking activities. Such 'short termism' is a common complaint laid against shareholders across sectors, but it is particularly serious in the banking sector. The reasons for this are twofold. First, banks are highly leveraged companies. The interests of shareholders are tiny compared with those of the depositors and the other creditors. Secondly, everyone assumes that banks – particularly the big ones – will be rescued if they get into trouble. The downside risk for the shareholders is, therefore, mitigated to some extent. The shareholders in RBS lost most of their money but, in risk terms, they should have lost all of it.

The risk reward equation for all equity investors was clear. If the bank succeeds in a risk-taking activity, the return on equity is magnified because of the bank's leverage. If it fails, the government will pick up the pieces and not all will be lost. This moral hazard continues to be a conundrum and will be until some mechanism is found to ensure that shareholders suffer appropriate losses when their investee banks take imprudent risks.

Faced with organisations which were too complicated for their managements and boards to control and shareholders who were out to maximise short-term returns, responsibility for the monitoring of the health of the banking sector fell on the regulators and the rating agencies. We have already seen that, the governmental adopted the view that 'light touch' regulation was all that was needed, so that there was a crying need for independent, fearless, competent rating agencies.

Unfortunately, as is well documented, the rating agencies did not spot the weaknesses either in the banks themselves or in the instruments in which the banks invested. For example, Moody's was still giving ratings of Aa1 to Royal Bank of Scotland and Bank of Scotland right up to their enforced rescues. Even with the implicit governmental support, these were optimistic ratings (and higher than these banks have received since). Worse still, the rating agencies' independence had been compromised because they had been liberal in giving AAA ratings to mortgage backed securities (often issued by and invested in by the banks) which were now looking anything but AAA. The very organisations which should have been the whistle-blowers, were implicated in their overenthusiasm for structured products (and from the fees associated with rating them).

None of these five lines of defence prevented some banks from taking risks which, even at the time seemed reckless and in hindsight, were obviously so.

Chapter 8

The Situation in 2008

By 2008, bankers were in an unprecedented situation. They were managing organisations, many of which were fearsomely complex, containing lending and trading businesses; equity and debt; customer businesses and proprietary trading. They were issuing complex securitisations and other types of structured finance which offloaded much of the issuer's risk, but other parts of the same bank were buying their competitors' issuers' issues which brought these risks straight back. Many bank senior managers were not fully qualified to manage such businesses but were being hugely rewarded for doing so. As long as earnings per share continued to grow, their reputations (and wallets) flourished but there was little incentive to control the risks that were being run. The conventional wisdom was that banks needed light regulation and had 'nailed' the problem of risk. Rapid growth was regarded as being consistent with controlled risk. Bankers were paid a lot, which worried some, but others regarded banking as one of the few industries where Britain was pre-eminent. They pointed to the fact that bankers had always been seen to be overpaid. For example, over a century ago Lord Keynes observed, 'How long will it be necessary to pay City men so entirely out of proportion to what other servants of society commonly receive for performing social services not less useful or difficult?'[97] Bankers were in the forefront of the economy and the banker as economic hero was not as ludicrous as it seems today. There were, admittedly, some egregious examples which attracted criticism – for example a group of half a dozen Barclays executives were sacked in 2002 for spending £ 44,000 on a celebratory dinner – but in general, there was little political opposition to high bankers' pay.

Customer care deteriorated in that customer business had ceased to be as important as hitherto; some banks began to resemble huge hedge funds where the bank was mainly run in order to make profits from trading 'on its own account' rather than providing a service to customers.

The banks' attitude towards customers with trading difficulties illustrates the point. Traditionally, the 'lead' clearing bank would organise a rescue package for the customer, with the dual aims of protecting good, long-term businesses and earning a good return to the banks. In the case of a large and complex reorganisation, the Bank of England would also become involved as a coordinator (the so-called London Approach). One of the most prominent of the 'work out' specialists was Stan Carslake, a famously tough 'intensive care' banker at Barclays in the 1980s.[98] He and his counterparts in the other clearing banks were aiming primarily at safeguarding the banks' assets, but also at protecting viable businesses and also earning a good return for the risks taken. Such an approach, which was in the interest of the customer, the lending bank and society at large, survived in part during the recession of the early nineties, though it was beginning to break down. Interestingly, it probably lasted longest in the two major Scottish clearing banks, who were highly regarded by industrialists for their supportive behaviour.

What a contrast with more recent behaviour by the same banks! RBS and its 'Global Restructuring Group' has been accused of deliberately weakening customers in order to enhance bank returns and the Financial Conduct Authority is still considering whether there is a basis to take action against RBS. While I have no direct evidence to support such a contention, I do have direct experience of RBS's approach to a customer, of which I was chairman. The Group had trading difficulties, but not insurmountable ones – an assessment shared by the company and RBS. Throughout the negotiations, the RBS workout unit made it clear that their sole objective was to maximise income to the bank, either in the form of fees or, ideally, equity in the company. The wellbeing of the company, its customers, shareholders, staff, management, suppliers, pensioners and other stakeholders were all irrelevant. The short-term interests of RBS were paramount, though as it turned out, the management were incompetent at achieving even this aim.

Such behaviour towards companies in difficulties did not appear to spread throughout all clearing banks but other customer unfriendly practices did become common. Examples of customer mistreatment have been the various incidents of mis-selling, the largest of which, the payment protection insurance (PPI) scandal, involved paying out £ 24.2 billion to customers between 2011 and January 2016, according to the *Guardian* website.[99] Other examples of malfeasance and inappropriate behaviour, such as LIBOR fixing, mis-selling of interest rate swaps and mis-selling of endowment mortgages show that PPI was not an isolated example of bad behaviour. Emma Dunkley in the Financial Times on 11 April 2016 pointed out that, 'Britain's banks and building societies have paid out almost £ 53 billion in fines and other penalties since 2000.'

It might be claimed that the bankers of earlier days also treated customers badly. While there may have been isolated instances of such behaviour (and there were widespread examples of cartels), it was not, in my experience, common to treat customers deliberately badly. Banks, stockbrokers and other financial service companies pre Big Bang generally held their clients in high regard and great effort was made to acquire and keep high quality clients and customers.[100] In 2012, a Goldman Sachs trader, Greg Smith, left the firm and published a book[101] which, among other things, claimed that there was a "toxic" culture where executives frequently referred to clients as "muppets".[102] Smith may or may not have exaggerated his ex-colleagues' behaviour but it is clear that calling clients 'muppets' was not an isolated incident. It is difficult to imagine a similar culture pervading Goldmans in earlier days when it was a partnership and when clients were cherished.

As I have explained above, the divorce from customers/clients has taken place both as regards personal and corporate business. The bank manager who used to know his/her customer has disappeared to be replaced by algorithms and call centres. The relationship officer, who used to look after the corporate customer and played a part in assessing the credit risk on the customer, has become more like a 'pure' salesperson, motivated and incentivised to sell as much product to the customer as possible. It is not at all surprising that these people have often been tempted to 'oversell' and encourage customers to engage in inappropriate transactions. On those occasions when the transaction is so complicated that the salesperson doesn't fully understand the deal, then the risks to the customer multiply.

Customers and bankers meet much less frequently than before, and customer business has become less important than hitherto (though of course it is still a very important component of most banks' activities). The challenge to bankers is to remember that, although direct customer contact will take place less frequently than before – that is the nature of modern banking – the quality of the relationship manager when personal contact *does* take place is all the more vital. Handelsbanken in their expansion of UK branch banking appear to have recognised this point.

Alongside the dilution of customer business, banks also forgot that they had a social as well as a commercial role. Until Big Bang, the various types of financial institution – clearing bank, merchant bank, building society, stockbroker, stockjobber, discount house, etc. – all had their own niches. Price and other agreements ensured that these different organisations could make a decent profit without needing to compete too viciously. The *quid pro quo* was that innovation was lacking and the bankers could carry on serving their traditional customer base – and having leisurely lunches. For example, women and 'working class' customers were particularly ill-served by the traditional clearing banks. However, banks, particularly the clearing banks, and the building societies did see themselves as providing a vital social purpose, as well as simply making money, even if their definition of 'society' was far too tightly drawn. It might be useful to remind ourselves of the Anthony Sampson quote on page 13, 'In their dedication, their lack of greed, and their sense of quiet service, the joint stock bankers (i.e. the clearing bankers) provide[d] a placid, safe centre to financial Britain.' The archetypal bank manager was portrayed by Arthur Lowe as Captain Mainwaring in *Dad's Army*; someone who was conservative by nature but knew his customers well and also knew the bank's role in the life of the town. Against these qualities, he may have been narrow minded and suspicious of change. It would be neither possible nor desirable to grow a cadre of modern day 'Mainwarings' but it is critical to re-establish bankers as highly regarded participants in society. Banking is too important a 'utility' to allow bankers to remain as pariahs, held in contempt by many of their customers.

The second part of this investigation attempts to assess how things have changed since 2008 and suggests ways in which, within current society, bankers can begin to be rehabilitated. But first, I shall try to explain in brief what happened in 2007/8.

Chapter 9

The Great Crash

By 2007 all the preconditions for a crash were in place. Bankers were prepared to lend on assets and to businesses which would, under normal circumstances, be regarded as too risky. Parts of the US 'sub-prime' market was a case in point. The film, *The Big Short*[103] showed bankers lending to people without predictable income and/or with payment difficulties and bad credit histories and at property valuations which were wildly optimistic. These loans were then 'packaged' – divided up into tranches to appeal to different buyers. The individual tranches were sold to banks and non – banks throughout the world. It goes without saying that many of these investors had no knowledge of the local markets where these mortgages were generated. Rather, they relied on the credit ratings which had been assigned to the loans by Agencies such as Standard and Poor's, Moody's and Fitch.

Such packaging was not harmful in itself but the bankers, based often on 'rose tinted' ratings from Credit Agencies, persuaded themselves that, even if the whole loan was very risky, the particular part of it which they had bought was not. Often the technical details of these packages were not fully understood by Boards, managements, traders or regulators. They also assumed that if things went wrong they could quickly sell their investment. This assumption might hold good for a single bank. It cannot be true for the whole market. Someone has to be holding the parcel when the music stops. Furthermore, many of these banks relied for much of their funding on short-term borrowing from the interbank market and ignored any possibility that this market might contract.

To make matters worse, the UK Regulator was pursuing a 'light touch' policy, encouraged by politicians of all sides which in the case of RBS led to '... a series of failures and misjudgements in supervision ranging from the failure to analyse and understand balance sheet risks relating to capital, liquidity and asset quality, to the decision not to interfere in RBS's calamitous acquisition of parts of ABN AMRO.'[104] Even though the preconditions for a crash were present in 2007 and probably had been present for some time and though the US sub-prime market had shown signs of weakness during the first half of 2007, it takes an incident or a combination of them to cause people to change their assumptions about the world and to precipitate a crash. The first of these incidents took place on 9 August 2007 when, according to Reuters '... BNP Paribas ... froze 1.6 billion euros ... worth of funds ... citing the U.S. subprime mortgage sector woes that have rattled financial markets worldwide.'[105]. Nevertheless, most market participants did not foresee BNP's action as the prelude to a crash. Reuters reported that other major banks and financial service companies had said that there was 'no cause for concern'.

Later that day everyone had cause for concern: the short-term money markets ceased to function. These markets had for decades successfully enabled banks to raise short-term money if they had a temporary shortage or to place temporary excesses. Their smooth operation depended upon the banks trusting each other to be able to repay these short-term loans at maturity and, although the maturities were often very short term – overnight or a matter of a few days – in the febrile atmosphere of August 2007 that trust had evaporated. This heightened sensitivity to credit and liquidity risk led to a reduction in banks' appetite to use the money market [106]and it became clear that there would be no rapid return to normal. Central Banks increased their advances to banks who needed these short-term funds. However, it also became evident that some institutions had been using the short-term money markets as funding for their long-term assets. By 14 September, Northern Rock was forced to apply to the Bank of England for liquidity support – and it was obvious that this support was unlikely to be short term in character. Despite this support, depositors in Northern Rock were not convinced that the bank was safe, and a run began on the bank, the first major run on a UK banking institution since Overend, Gurney failed in 1866. In particular, those depositors with large deposits (over £ 35,000 at that time) could not rely on the Financial Services Compensation Scheme to protect themselves fully. An estimated £ 2 billion had been withdrawn by the following Monday, 17 September, at which point the government announced that they would guarantee all Northern Rock's deposits. Unsuccessful attempts were then made to sell the business but on 17 February 2008 the Chancellor of the Exchequer, Alistair Darling, announced that Northern Rock was to be nationalised, claiming that the private bids did not offer 'sufficient value for money to the taxpayer'[107] and thus the bank was to be brought under a temporary period of public ownership.

Meanwhile, RBS continued to grow rapidly. Pre-tax profits rose from £ 6.9 billion in 2004 to £ 7.9 billion in 2005 and £ 9.2 billion in 2006[108]. In 2006, the bank decided to expand its structured credit business worldwide. On 18 April 2007, RBS (in concert with Fortis Bank and Santander Bank) put in a proposal to acquire ABN AMRO, a major European bank, and later in the month, Barclays came up with a competing offer. RBS received due diligence information in April, obtained overwhelming shareholder approval for the acquisition in August and completed the transaction in mid October, following the withdrawal of Barclays' bid earlier in the month. From the outside it appeared that the ABN AMRO acquisition – at the time, the largest takeover in banking history – was the latest triumph in Fred Goodwin's career, but in truth cracks were beginning to appear in the RBS edifice. First, the due diligence which had been done on ABN AMRO was superficial: in the words of the FSA Chairman, 'Many readers of the report will be startled to read that the information made available to RBS by ABN AMRO in April 2007 amounted to "two lever arch folders and a CD".'[109] Admittedly, due diligence for acquisitions of public companies is necessarily limited but the ABN AMRO case does seem to have been extreme. I was told that on acquisition and for some time afterwards, RBS did not know their total groupwide exposure to major counterparties. Secondly, as noted above, RBS had decided to expand its 'structured credit' business in 2006, not long before the US sub-prime market began to show signs of strain. By August 2007, when negotiations on the ABN AMRO takeover were in full flow, RBS's own models were showing significant risks in their credit portfolio. And thirdly, as also noted above, the money markets had seized up in the same month. Yet the RBS management and board pressed on regardless. Just a few weeks after the ABN AMRO acquisition was completed in October 2007, the FSA added RBS to its 'watchlist' of banks which needed special attention. At a Christmas dinner given for bank senior managers, Fred Goodwin was sitting next to the wife of an RBS senior manager who asked him about the implications of the money market collapse and the run on Northern Rock. Goodwin remained very optimistic on the prospects for RBS.

During the early days of 2008, indicators were mixed. In February, RBS declared a pre-tax profit of £ 9.9 billion for 2007, up from £ 9.2 billion in the previous year. However, in the same month, the FSA and Goodwin had agreed that the bank's capital position was tight and in April 2008, RBS announced that it would be raising £ 12 billion of capital through a rights issue. Despite this capital raising effort and a new Special Liquidity Scheme introduced by the Bank of England in the same month[110], RBS's share price was in free fall. During the summer, RBS and other major UK banks found it more difficult to raise money in the wholesale interbank markets and in July, RBS announced a loss for the half year of £ 691 million, after 'credit market write-downs of £ 5.9 billion'[111]. In September, the pressure increased still further. In the month, Lehmann Brothers filed for bankruptcy; Fortis Bank (a major Benelux bank and a co-bidder with RBS for part of the ABN AMRO business) had to be bailed out by its home governments; Lloyds Bank and HBOS merged (see below) and Washington Mutual, an active investor in US mortgage products, collapsed. Right at the end of the month, the Irish Government announced that they would guarantee deposits in six major banks, thereby putting pressure on those weak banks in other countries which benefitted from no such explicit guarantee. RBS suffered withdrawals of large corporate deposits and on 6 October, Standard and Poor's finally downgraded RBS's credit rating. The stage was set for the failure of RBS. As *The Telegraph* reported: 'On that Tuesday morning, [7 October] RBS shares crashed 20pc as what little confidence remaining, evaporated on rumours of a run. With nowhere else to turn and fearing imminent failure, Sir Tom McKillop, RBS chairman, put a desperate call through to the Treasury. Alistair Darling, the Chancellor, had taken an early flight to Luxembourg that day for the Ecofin meeting. His aides pulled him out of his meeting and a room was cleared to take the call'.[112] The Bank of England had the ability to lend to RBS but only if they believed that the bank was solvent and, reasonably, they were not confident that this was so. Work had been going on for several weeks on a recapitalisation plan for RBS and other British banks, but it was only in the afternoon of that day that the outline plan was agreed. It was sufficient for the Bank of England to agree to providing the liquidity which RBS so desperately needed.

At its peak, the UK Government provided £ 256 billion of facilities for RBS,[113] comprising £ 202 billion of support under the Asset Protection Scheme and £ 54 billion of actual or committed capital. The FSA's report into the failure of RBS, when eventually produced in December 2011, adduced seven reasons for the bank's failure, namely:[114]

» RBS's capital position and the underlying regulatory framework

» RBS's liquidity position

» Asset quality: concerns and uncertainties

» Losses in credit trading activities

» ABN AMRO acquisition: 'the wrong price, the wrong way to pay, at the wrong time and the wrong deal'

» Systemic vulnerabilities and confidence collapse: failure of the banks in worse relative positions

» Management, governance and culture

The FSA also criticised its own supervisory approach, priorities and resources. It is not too cynical to wonder which aspects of RBS's business model and governance *were* satisfactory.

While the government's actions saved RBS and with it the UK banking sector, it left a seriously, perhaps fatally, wounded institution. Over the 10 years since the rescue, RBS has failed to turn in a consistently profitable performance. It is a 'zombie bank' which would, I believe, have been broken up and its constituent parts sold were it not for the government wishing to recover its investment in RBS at some stage. The government had a legitimate, essential role in rescuing RBS in 2008. Keeping the bank as a nationalised industry for a decade is not justified.

If RBS was a long-term tragedy, Lloyds' failure came as the result of a single disastrous decision to buy HBOS. Lloyds had had a reputation as a cautious, rather stodgy, bank for some years; it did not join with the enthusiasm of others in the moves towards large investment banking businesses or aggressive property and other lending. HBOS on the other hand, since the merger between Halifax and Bank of Scotland in 2001, had followed an increasingly adventurous path. By the start of 2006 '... the exposure to commercial property, ... was 52%, or £ 44bn of the corporate loan book ... and [this] had risen to 56% by the end of 2008. There was also exposure to 'single names', with the top 30 largest exposures accounting for 15% of the portfolio in 2006, rising to 23% by the end of March 2008.[115] Despite warnings from the FSA, pointing out deficiencies in credit management and processes and the resignation of Paul Moore, Head of Risk, in 2004[116], the bank's corporate lending activities under Peter Cummings was allowed to expand rapidly. When the bad market news began to percolate through in 2008, HBOS came under pressure. In July, it announced that its first half profits had fallen by almost three quarters and that month it raised £ 4 billion through a rights issue in order to boost capital. As the banking markets deteriorated, HBOS's shares suffered from 'short selling' where investors gained from any fall in its share price.

Lloyds then announced that it planned to take over HBOS in September 2008. On 17 September 2008, encouraged by the government, which waived competition requirements to allow the acquisition to go ahead, Lloyds agreed takeover terms with HBOS were announced. Lloyds saw HBOS as an opportunity to increase their UK market at a stroke while paying way under what they thought was its market value. The government regarded Lloyds as the rescuer of HBOS, thereby relieving it of a potential problem. The error of these views was soon evident. Within a few weeks, Lloyds itself, regarded as one of the most stable banks before its HBOS adventure, had to accept new capital from the government and became, in effect, nationalised.

Within a year, RBS and Lloyds had passed into government hands and another – Bradford & Bingley – had been nationalised. The Alliance and Leicester had been bought by Santander Bank in October 2008 and government loans had been made to a number of other banks, UK and Icelandic, and to the Financial Services Compensation Scheme in order to ensure that no UK retail depositor lost money[117]. In all, the government support at its peak amounted to £ 1,162 billion. To put that figure in context – it is approximately equivalent to an average £ 20,000 for each person in the UK. The sector which had been the pride of successive governments appeared to be in danger of beggaring the population. Ten years later, the effects of the bailout of the UK banking sector are still being felt.

PART II

Chapter 1

Banking since 2008

The rescue of RBS, Lloyds/HBOS, Northern Rock, Bradford and Bingley and others in 2008 produced such an upwelling of justifiable criticism of the banking sector that there was a political imperative that 'something must be done' about the banks. Indeed, there have been some positive developments, along the following lines:

1. Capital requirements have been increased markedly.

2. The 'straightforward' UK commercial banking activities of major banks are in the process of being 'ring-fenced' from their investment banking activities, as recommended by the Independent Commission on Banking, chaired by Sir John Vickers. The rationale for this proposal is that a failure in the (perceived higher risk) investment banking part of the bank should not 'infect' the commercial banking part of the business.

3. Certain types of bond finance for banks, such as contingent capital instruments (CoCos) will be 'bailed-in' in the case of the bank encountering difficulties (i.e. on the occurrence of certain events the bonds will be converted from debt to equity, thereby strengthening the bank's capital base at a time of need).

4. The FSA has been replaced by two regulatory authorities. First the PRA (Prudential Regulation Authority), part of the Bank of England, which has responsibility for ensuring that banks

are run in a prudent manner and second the FCA (Financial Conduct Authority) which has responsibility for trying to ensure that banks do not behave badly and that they treat customers fairly.

5. The introduction of the 'Senior Managers' Regime' (SMR) has identified the individual responsibilities of senior executives and non-executives and provided a structure under which the individuals can be held legally responsible for serious failures. (One of the aspects of the 2008 debacle which caused most dismay was that no-one appeared to be called to account for the failures.)

6. The Walker Report (2009)[118] recommended a number of governance changes, notably improvements in the recruiting, training and time involvement of non-executive directors, in particular, as they relate to the risk process; better disclosure on pay and a move away from short-term incentives and closer involvement by institutional shareholders in monitoring the banks' performance. Most of these recommendations have been adopted.

It is fair to say that these measures individually and together have improved the banking environment, though at a large cost in terms of regulators and compliance staff. More capital has improved bank stability and the PRA and FCA are 'steadier hands' than the FSA used to be. There are occasional problems with the two regulatory organisations giving different 'steers'. Also 'Treating Customers Fairly'- a justifiable concern of the FCA – can sometimes seem to be interpreted as 'Treating Customers the Same'. The FCA is more bureaucratic than the PRA and the burden of regulation has increased, but the system feels more stable than in the years leading up to 2008. Ring-fencing may also help in certain circumstances, though it may hinder in others. For example, it could be used to isolate a healthy investment banking business from a failing commercial banking one. It is worthwhile pointing out that while many of the problems in 2008 were due to major investment banking losses, there were also large problems within some 'traditional' commercial banks.

The introduction of the SMR equally may be a double-edged sword. It may, as Martin Wheatley (the former FCA Chief Executive) noted, be used to '… [give] clarity on rules that will embed personal accountability into the culture of The City.'[119] On the other hand, the fact that non-executive directors are now held to account for their areas of responsibility may result in those non-executives losing their independence of the executives. CoCos also may have unpredictable effects. As pointed out by Martin Taylor,[120] investors may 'flip' from 'believing all issuers equally safe to thinking many equally precarious when the sky next darkens'.

Overall then the situation seems a little more stable than in 2008, if still precarious. Until interest rates can be reinstated at levels which give a proper return to investment and the banks finish clearing out their toxic and difficult to value assets, the banking system cannot be said to have normalised.

However, there are more fundamental problems with banks than those which can be rectified by better regulation, more capital, sensible interest rates and asset clear ups. They involve the relationship between banks/bankers and their customers and the position that banks fulfil in society.

In considering these points, it is important to try to define these relationships. For example, it is sometimes said that the banks are no longer trusted. Yet people happily entrust their liquid assets to the banks and seem to show few signs of distress in doing so. For the vast majority of these deposits (those under £ 85,000), there is insurance which guarantees that the depositor will not lose money. For the larger deposits, where there was any lack of trust, e.g. in Northern Rock, a run developed, and the bank was quickly rescued. In the case of RBS, it was the prospect of the bank having insufficient liquidity without a run having taken place which persuaded the authorities to take rapid action. In fact, the experience of the last decade supports the idea that deposits in any bank, however badly run, will be safe. Depositors in those Icelandic Banks which failed earned a comparatively high rate of interest (to reflect the higher risk they were running) and were then paid out in full when the failures occurred. There is nothing in recent history to suggest that deposits in banks large or small are in any way unsafe. Accordingly, people behave as if they trust these institutions.

What has happened is that bank customers no longer trust their banker to act in a helpful and reasonable manner. They suspect, often with good reason, that the banker is behaving in a certain way because his or her bonus is dependent upon it. And, in this special sense, trust and respect have broken down. It should be noted that the traditional banker was not a saint either. Links between banks, insurance companies, estate agents and others often led to the customer overpaying for banking services. Nevertheless, encouraging customers to engage in transactions which were against their interests was, I suggest, much less prevalent. In part, this is because modern financial services are so complex that it is sometimes difficult to predict what *is* in the customer's interests. However, it is also because it is in the individual banker's direct pecuniary interest to sell aggressively the bank's products to their customers.

CASE STUDY: SWAPS FOR SMALL AND MEDIUM SIZED COMPANIES (SMEs)

Over the next few pages I use the mis-selling of swaps to SMEs as a case in point. As interest rates came down, banks realised that they could persuade many of their customers to 'lock in' those lower rates by engaging in interest rate swaps. The risk of rising interest rates was thereby eliminated. These products began to be sold in large numbers to small and medium sized businesses at the turn of the century and reached maximum volume in the years leading up to 2008. They were hugely profitable products for the banks. According to the FSA, it is estimated that over 28,000 interest rate swap agreements were sold to businesses across the UK by the four major banks.[121]

Suppose that a company had borrowed from the bank at an interest rate linked to six months LIBOR. Under these swaps, the customer might agree to receive from the bank 6-month LIBOR every six months. In return, the company would pay a fixed rate of interest of, say, 6% p.a. every six months. The company has thereby transformed a loan which was linked to LIBOR to one which was fixed at 6% (plus margin). A loan whose interest rate could fluctuate in either direction was in this way changed into a fixed rate one.

This could have been a good deal for many companies – and would have been had the swaps exactly matched the loan in amount and maturity and had interest rates not collapsed in a way which neither the customers (nor I suspect most of their bankers) expected. The problems in essence were fivefold:

1. 'Banks offering loans to SME customers often included a condition that required businesses to enter into interest rate swaps. The nominal value of the swap was often for much greater amounts and over a longer term than was necessary given the amount and term of the loan.'[122]

2. There was little attempt to assess the suitability of these products for the particular customer concerned.

3. Selling was often aggressive, giving the customer little time or opportunity to consider properly the advantages and disadvantages of the deal offered.

4. The banks often did not point out the consequences of a major, prolonged fall in interest rates. For example, many of these swaps were secured on cash or other assets. As interest rates plummeted, the banks demanded more and more security in order to support these swaps. Many customers could not find enough security and the swaps were terminated, often at huge costs to the customer. Some customers were bankrupted as a result.

5. The salespeople were usually from the retail bank side of the business and in many cases, they had little technical knowledge of the swaps product.

It may be instructive to see how this product might have been dealt with by a bank which was aware of its responsibilities to its customers and to society. It is an ethical, not a legal analysis. I assume (which I believe to be the case) that the banks in general believed that the swaps they sold to their customers were likely to be of benefit to those customers. They were not expecting a fall in interest rates of the degree and duration which occurred.

The first point to note is that when the banks offering loans to SME customers included a condition that required the customer to enter into interest rate swaps, this immediately gave the bank a moral obligation to the customer. The bank possesses the product knowledge and it should be up to the bank to take reasonable care to offer appropriate products to that customer. If we bought a lock with key, we would be surprised if, when we got home, the key didn't fit.

Secondly, it should have been stressed by the bank that a swap which exactly matches the customer's loan in maturity and amount is a very different product from one which does not match. The first carries some types of risks, particularly those associated with early maturities and security valuations (see below) but if both loan and swap continue to maturity, it does ensure that the customer has, in effect, borrowed at a known fixed interest rate. (Of course, if, as occurred, interest rates fell steeply, the fixed interest rate may appear very high. It is important to make it pellucidly clear to the customer that the swap achieves a known interest rate, not necessarily a cheap one.)

Selling swaps which are much longer maturity and much bigger than the underlying loan has all the risks above and, in addition, is a naked gamble taken by the customer; this should have been explained at the outset. The consequences of the gamble going wrong should have also been explained and it was wrong to put pressure on the customer to take such risks.

It appears that, not only did the banks not explain the various risks clearly, but they also put pressure on their customers to do deals quickly and spent little time considering whether the swap was appropriate for that particular customer at that particular time. Clearly such behaviour is unacceptable, and it is right that the banks have been criticised and fined for it. It is not clear that the companies adversely affected have been properly compensated for their losses.

Suppose for a moment, however, that the swap sold was suited to the customer and the same size and maturity of the loan. Nobody expected interest rates to fall to near zero and stay there for so long. So, in such circumstances, what would be the bank's responsibilities?

One critical point is how the swap was sold to the customer. If it was the customer's own initiative and decision and the customer was a financially sophisticated individual or organisation, then it is difficult to think that the bank has any responsibility to compensate the customer. However, if the swap was actively 'sold' to the customer by the bank and, especially, if the taking out of the swap was linked formally to a loan or other transaction, then perhaps the bank should share in the 'pain', particularly if the customer was not familiar with swap structures and risks.

Note that the banks' sales pitches stressed the certainty of taking out a swap and the advantages of a swap if interest rates went up, but frequently didn't point out that if interest rates went down and stayed down, the swapped in interest rate could appear very high. In these circumstances, there is a case for saying that the bank has a moral duty to share in the loss suffered.

Unfortunately, as indicated above, the disadvantages of swap transactions were sometimes more serious. Where swaps were taken out by small and medium sized businesses the bank often took security against these transactions in the form of cash, property or other assets. If the value of the swap to the bank increases, such that the amount the customer has to pay to the bank over time is greater than the amount the bank expects to pay to the customer, then the bank can claim greater security. Suppose, for example, that the customer has a £ 1 million, 10–year swap with the bank where the customer receives LIBOR from the bank and pays the bank 6% per annum. Suppose also that LIBOR has fallen to 1% per annum. Every year the customer pays a net £ 50,000 to the bank (6% minus 1% on £ 1 million). Over the 10-year period of the swap the customer will have paid over £ 500,000 (assuming interest rates stay the same). The bank might ask for security of say £ 700,000 to cover that amount owed with some allowance for safety. The customer may not have that security and may not have reasonably expected such a large demand to be made. Equally, the bank may not have expected such a fall in interest rates and a consequential need for to demand security. Clearly, if the customer can afford the extra security, they should pay up: it is a financial obligation and one which should be honoured if possible. However, what about the situation where the customer has insufficient security available and/or providing the bank with security would prevent the customer from using that security for important corporate purposes. Doesn't the bank have a responsibility to moderate its security demands and try to help the customer trade through a problem for which the bank in part has unwittingly been responsible?

Instead of taking such a collegiate view of financial responsibilities, there have been some banks, notably RBS, who have deliberately made demands of their customers in order to extract fees and equity positions from those customers.

Whereas some customers are financially very sophisticated, others need considerable guidance through complex financial transactions. The swaps business is one where neither the banks nor their customers foresaw some of the drawbacks of these instruments. These difficulties having occurred, the banks should have worked with their customers to try to mitigate the problems. The fact that they didn't and in some cases allegedly made those problems worse, indicates that the banks really haven't learnt their lessons.

The swaps episode suggests 5 ways in which the banks should have corrected their behaviour:

1. Selling should have been less aggressive.

2. Customers should not have been persuaded to take out swaps much bigger and longer than the underlying loans, i.e. to mismatch loans and swaps.

3. Customers should not have been pressured into deciding quickly (these transactions are complex and even the banks themselves, as it turns out, hadn't thought through all the implications).

4. The banks should have considered sharing in the pain where they had actively sold swaps to customers.

5. The banks should have considered relaxing security and other requirements where customers were finding it difficult to meet security demands.

In these ways the bankers would be, and would be seen to be, taking the customers side and helping them to succeed. Note, I am not suggesting, where the customer has taken a considered, knowledgeable decision that that customer should escape the consequences of their action. To take another example, suppose a customer decided to take a 6% 5-year fixed rate loan at a time when this looked a good deal. There was no bank pressure to take out this loan. Unexpectedly, interest rates fell and stayed down, so that the customer had much higher interest costs than their competitors. As a result, profits suffered.

In these circumstances, the bank has no moral or legal obligation to help the customer out, unless those losses become 'life threatening' for the business. In that case, I believe that the bank should examine the situation and see if, by granting forbearance to the customer, that the customer's position could be improved. (Of course, if the bank had encouraged or pressurised the customer to take out the fixed rate loan, then, just as in the swaps case, the bank has a moral duty to consider whether it should share in the financial 'pain' suffered by the customer.)

END OF CASE STUDY

The above case study concerns swap transactions. The same points could be made *mutatis mutandis* with a number of other types of transaction such as PPIs (payment protection insurance), LIBOR determination, and the practice of dealing with companies in difficulties. In all these cases, banks have been guilty of behaving badly. I shall try below to analyse the duties of a bank in a more generalised way, without specifying the nature of the deal. Several questions of an ethical nature arise, depending on the situation. Suppose first that the bank had encouraged the customer to do the deal, or in extreme cases, had specified that the deal be done.

1. Why should banks have a moral duty to compensate their customers when things go wrong, while other suppliers of goods and services accept no such liability even if they aggressively sell the deal?

2. If the deal goes in the customer's favour, there is no 'sharing of the spoils'; why, therefore, should the bank offer to share in the losses?

3. If the bank does choose to help a customer in distress, what kind of financial return should it accept for doing so?

4. Perhaps the overarching question, why should a privately owned organisation, such as a bank, act otherwise than in the long-term interests of its shareholders?

One answer to the first question is that suppliers often do go beyond their legal duty in rectifying unforeseen problems. For example, I was recently at the theatre when the performance had to be stopped near the end. The theatre was under no obligation to offer refunds or tickets for other performances but, of course, did so. Many restaurants offer vouchers to those who have had bad experiences (though this naturally assumes that the diner wants to repeat the experience!). Nevertheless, there is a difference. A bank compensating for an error or for unknowingly misleading a customer might have to pay away very large amounts of money, not simply the price of a meal or a theatre ticket. Perhaps the bank should have been much more careful in what it said but the question remains, 'Why should a bank compensate customers if they don't have a clear legal obligation to do so?' The point is considered in more detail below.

Of course, sometimes the customer gains more than expected as a result of deals done at the bank's urging. In those cases, the bank does not share in the 'upside'. Isn't that a little unfair if the bank is expected to bear some of the losses? The critical point here is that the bank has tried to persuade the customer of the wisdom of doing this particular transaction. Even if the bank is not offering formal 'advice' it is clear that the bank, as an expert, believes this to be a correct course of action. It is not unreasonable to expect, therefore, that the bank should share in the downside but not in the upside. The point is much stronger where the bank has 'tied' the doing of one deal to another.

If the bank decides to help a customer who, by entering into the transaction has suffered serious adverse financial consequences, to what extent should the bank be rewarded for giving that help? This depends, in my view, on precisely the circumstances of the transaction. The bank should be properly rewarded and, given that the customer is in financial stress, that return can be considerable. The determinants of an appropriate reward should be:

a. The degree of persuasion exercised by the bank in encouraging the customer to do the deal in the first place.

b. The current financial state of the customer.

It seems perfectly reasonable that the bank should share in the recovery of the company, assuming that such equity share is not too generous and does not distort the bank's (or the banker's) motivations. It is important that the bank's principal aim should be the financial health of the customer leading to the recovery of its own exposure to the customer. The bank's return should be a secondary consideration. The bank should embrace the idea of sharing in the success or failure of its customer. Unfortunately, the behaviour of some of the clearing banks fell woefully short of these standards in the years leading up to 2008.

But the most fundamental question is, 'Why should banks ever act otherwise than in the long-term interests of their shareholders?' It may of course be the case that the customer friendly behaviour I have outlined normally *is* in the long-term shareholder interest and I believe that this is often so. Nevertheless, suppose that it is not. I remain convinced that banks and bankers should adopt a collegiate approach to their customers.

Banks form a unique group of institutions in our society. Their continued existence relies on confidence and it has been shown that they can and do depend on state aid in difficult times.

That state aid may come in the form of short-term liquidity lines from the Bank of England or, as in the cases of RBS, Lloyds, Northern Rock and Bradford and Bingley, state ownership in whole or in part. As noted above, state aid to RBS and Lloyds at its peak exceeded £ 500 billion. For the banking system as a whole, support reached over £ 1 trillion at its highest point.[123] RBS in particular is still not consistently profitable nearly 10 years after the banking crisis. The authorities would love this state support to wither away but no one believes that it will. Another banking crisis tomorrow and the state would have to step in again. The worthwhile reforms which have been put in place since 2008 (see page 91 et seq.) have reduced the chance of future failures but have not made a serious difference to the likely reaction to such a failure.

Other types of organisations may also need state rescues – some utility providers are cases in point – but these are very different situations from banks. It is difficult to conceive of a circumstance where a failing water company's operation would not be picked up by another water company. So, a government rescue, were it to occur, would not be likely to last long. Contrast the rescue of RBS which has now lasted for almost 10 years. This huge, complex financial institution has proved impossible to sell in the short term – at least at any price which satisfies the government. Furthermore, a utility rescue would be of a manageable size. RBS when rescued in 2008, had assets of over £ 2,000 billion. Although this compares apples with oranges it may be interesting to note that in the same year the GNP of the United Kingdom was around £ 500 billion. The biggest banks rivalled major economies in size and their near failure led to real sacrifices by the inhabitants of those countries where the banks happened to be located. Banks, their host governments and citizens of the host country, are locked in a mutual relationship which they need to recognise.

Given the above, it is difficult to argue that the banks should look only to the interests of their shareholders and can, in practice, ignore their responsibilities to society as long as they follow law and regulation. The truth is very different. Banks benefit from their unique position in society and, in return, have a clear responsibility to their customers, counterparties and suppliers as well as to society as a whole. (Utility companies have similar responsibilities, although the financial consequences of failing in those responsibilities are likely to be much smaller than with banks.) An ex-colleague of mine has pointed out that, whereas in most industries the demise of a competitor is good news, in the banking industry it most definitely is not. Even if you haven't lent directly to the affected bank, you have probably lent to banks which have exposures to the affected bank at one or more stages removed. The failure of one bank threatens the stability of the many.

There have been one or two indications that bank managements have begun to recognise those responsibilities in recent years. Anthony Jenkins was appointed as CEO of Barclays Bank in 2012 and, *inter alia*, was given the task of addressing the bank's 'toxic culture'.[124] Barclays was a bank based on strong, Quaker traditions which, under the leadership of Bob Diamond and others and in a dash to compete with the largest commercial and investment banks, seemed to adopt a very different and ruthless approach to business … The appointment of Jenkins was meant to signal a return to Barclays' more traditional strengths of customer care and ethical behaviour. He stressed the importance of staff supporting voluntary organisations – and gave them time off to do so. He reinforced the importance of customer care. Unfortunately, the investors, and therefore the board, were unconvinced that Jenkins' overall approach to strategy was in their long-term interest and he was sacked in 2015.

The Worshipful Company of International Bankers[125] has published the following principles, the Lord George Principles for Good Business Conduct, which were developed in 2004 at the initiative of the late Eddie George, ex-Governor of the Bank of England:

1. To act honestly and fairly at all times when dealing with clients, customers and counterparties and to be a good steward of their interests, taking into account the nature of the business relationship with each of them, the nature of the service to be provided to them and the individual mandates given by them.

2. To act with integrity in fulfilling the responsibilities of your appointment and seek to avoid any acts or omissions or business practices which damage the reputation of your organisation and the financial services industry.

3. To observe applicable law, regulations and professional conduct standards when carrying out financial service activities and to interpret and apply them according to principles rooted in trust, honesty and integrity.

4. To observe the standards of market integrity, good practice and conduct required by or expected of participants in markets when engaged in any form of market dealings.

5. To be alert to and manage fairly and effectively and to the best of your ability any relevant conflict of interest.

6. To attain and actively manage a level of professional competence appropriate to your responsibilities, to commit to continued learning to ensure the currency of your knowledge, skills and expertise and to promote the development of others.

7. To decline any engagement for which you are not competent unless you have access to such advice and assistance as will enable you to carry out the work competently.

8. To strive to uphold the highest personal and professional standards.[126]

These are sound principles and they should be followed by all professional bankers – and indeed by all professional business people. If they had been followed by bankers, many of the egregious practices of the industry would, no doubt, have been prevented. However, there are aspects of banks which need to be changed even if all bankers followed Lord George's precepts.

My contention is that banks are different and should be treated as such. As noted by the International Bank for Reconstruction and Development, 'Banks are different from the generality of companies in that their collapse affects a far wider circle of people and, moreover, may undermine the financial system itself, with dire effects for the whole economy. This places a special responsibility upon a bank's directors'.[127] Even though systemic effects can be reduced by reforms such as those recommended in the Vickers Report (see page 91 above) it is not possible to eliminate the chance that the failure of one bank will spread to others.

Banks are also different in that (because of the dire effects noted above) they can expect special help from the authorities if they experience liquidity or even solvency problems. As the Parliamentary Commission on Banking Standards states,[128] 'Bank boards face particular challenges and responsibilities compared to other organisations. These primarily reflect the systemic risks associated with banking, and also specific regulatory requirements to mitigate conduct risk. As a result of their "too important to fail" status, banks benefit from an implicit subsidy … This implicit subsidy – based upon the expectation of taxpayer support – has led to significant taxpayer bailouts of some banks as well as other forms of support to the banking sector as a whole.' That doesn't mean that banks can't be public companies (or private ones) but that they should govern themselves in a way which reflects their public duty and the benefits they receive from civil society by virtue of being recognised banks. The liquidity and, on occasion, shareholding support from which banks benefit should be balanced by a recognition that banks have a special set of duties to their customers, namely:

» Banking services are complex and many customers do not fully understand them.

» Neither do many of the bankers who are charged with selling them to the public.

» From this it follows that a) Bankers should be circumspect about selling new products to customers and b) If things go wrong, they should try to help the customer.

» The extent of that help should depend on the extent to which the bank 'sold' the product and the ability of the customer to assess the product.

» The customer's wellbeing should be in the forefront of the banker's mind at all times.

Some bankers might claim that this is a doctrine of perfection and that no real bank follows these precepts. In my view that is wrong. I have worked for organisations which do put the interests of customers first and where this principle underlies everything they do. It is not an impossible dream. Some banks, for example, Handelsbanken, say that they aspire to these standards and my conversations with a few of their customers suggest that they are making laudable attempts to do so. I also think that there are many people working within the banking system who try diligently to work in this way. There are also many who are out for themselves and others who are jobsworths and bureaucrats. The failure of bank managements has been implicitly to encourage the greedy and the apparatchiks and to de-emphasise the customer aspects of the business. It should be added that regulation has not been helpful in promoting true customer service. For example, the 'Treating Customers Fairly' policy has in some cases led to 'Treating Customers the Same' and not to recognising that some customers have particular needs and treating them accordingly.

Bankers also might claim that the kind of customer service detailed above is incompatible with banks' obligations to their shareholders. That may be true under current company law, although I have a feeling that banks who truly care about their customers will be those who eventually generate the most shareholder value. In any event, there is no reason why there should not be an amendment to the Companies Act to reflect banks' peculiar role in society. The 2006 Companies Act (the 'Act') already includes a clause which attempts to put all companies under an obligation to consider the effects of their actions on stakeholders, not just shareholders. This clause, Number s172(1), reads as follows:

'A director of a company must act in a way that he considers, in good faith, would be most likely to promote the success of the company for the benefit of its members as a whole, and in doing so, have regard (amongst other matters) to –

a. The likely consequences of any decisions in the long term

b. The interests of the company's employees

c. The need to foster the company's business relationships with suppliers, customers and others

d. The impact of the company's operations on the community and the environment

e. The desirability of the company maintaining a reputation for high standards of business conduct, and

f. The need to act fairly between the members of the company.'[129]

As Professor Keay notes in 'The Duty to Promote the Success of the Company: is it fit for Purpose?', '… s 172 is not fit for purpose. … the provision does not fulfil the aims of the Government and we cannot have any confidence that it is going to address the problems with directors that have come to light in the wake of the financial crisis.'[130] The situation appears to be as before the Act, i.e. '... directors will consider stakeholder interests as far as they promote the success of the company, but only where it will benefit ... shareholders'.[131] It is difficult to disagree with Professor Keay's observation, particularly as it applies to banks. Where there is a 'trade-off' between long-term shareholder interest and those of other stakeholders, the perceived shareholders interest always seems to prevail. Several boards of banks appeared to disregard elements of Section 172 in the years leading up to – and after – the financial crisis, yet (as far as I am aware) no bank director has been charged with offences under the Act.

Although Section 172 has been ineffective, I do not see this as a reason to abandon all attempts to hold bank directors to legal obligations to their non-shareholder stakeholders. (I am not putting forward any views in relation to directors of non-bank companies.)

My argument is that, because banks are favourably treated by society (for good reason), bank boards should respond by being held to high community standards. Their responsibilities to customers, suppliers and staff should rank alongside those to shareholders and, in particular, their standards of customer care should not fall below given levels. Such responsibilities could be enshrined in a 'souped-up' Section 172 which obliges bank directors to consider the interests of all stakeholders and to act in accordance with the overall benefit to shareholders and other stakeholders taken as a whole.

If such a strengthened Section 172 were introduced, how in practice could bank boards of directors be held to such standards? Two possible formulations might be considered. 1) There could be the ability for customers to sue under the expanded Section 172 and/or 2) representatives of the customers (and possibly of other stakeholders) should be able to sit on bank boards, alongside directors who would continue to have responsibility to maximise shareholder value.

Of these two possibilities I strongly lean to the first. I think that banks should have the legal duty to treat customers properly and that if they fail in this duty they should be subject to the law. The second option, which would mean putting directors on bank boards who have differing interests, seems to me to be asking for trouble. There would be the risk that the boards fragmented into different interest groups, with the consequential difficulties of reaching collegiate solutions. Furthermore, it is unlikely that the 'customer directors' would form a large proportion of the total board, raising the possibility that this faction would be regularly outvoted. Better, I believe, to have a united board with a legal duty to represent all stakeholders and to weigh the interests of these different groups against each other before taking a decision.

A proposal to empower non-shareholder stakeholders will no doubt be unpopular within the banks and the investment community. There will be claims that banks will not be able to raise money if their objectives are more complex than that of maximising shareholder value. I disagree. As I note in page 74 above banks (and many other plc's) are very short term orientated, influenced by the short-term horizons of their institutional shareholders. A change in company law, ensuring that bank boards formally take into account the wellbeing of some (specified) stakeholders, will I think, lead to longer term policies which will benefit shareholders as well.

After all, under the current law and practice, the share price performance of British clearing banks since the Millenium has been spectacularly bad. The following is a guide, having made adjustments for stock splits:

Clearing Bank Share Prices[132]

	Approx. Price 2000 (p)	Recent Price (p)
Barclays	394.00 (17.12.99)	206.99 (02.8.17)
RBS	3538.20 (17.12.99)	250.80 (02.8.17)
Lloyds	483.33 (17.12.99)	65.26 (02.8.17)
HSBC	849.00 (19.12.99)	765.30 (02.8.17)

It is difficult to imagine a banking system with a more formal duty on banks to behave well producing a worse performance for investors than the system which has prevailed over the last 17 years. Investors should welcome a more community based banking system.

The last few paragraphs have concentrated on a change to the Companies Act, insofar as it affects banks, which may become necessary if bankers do not recognise, in practice, their duty to society. Such a change would not be necessary or would become otiose if bankers as a group decided to improve their behaviour of their own volition. The following are some areas where they might start:

» Bank branches: It is clear that branch usage has gone down, and no doubt will continue to do so. Yet, as pointed out by Martin Vander Weyer there are still many people for whom the closure of the local bank branch represents a real inconvenience. Banks should give more thought to ways 'that help branches stay viable.'[133]

» Bankers or Call Centres: When a customer rings a bank or visits a branch, they should be able to talk to an interested, informed banker who has their wellbeing at heart. **An example of perhaps how not to do it appeared on *Money Box* recently.**[134] An elderly customer had been deceived by a fraudster into making many large payments from his account. The bank was suspicious and read out a warning to him on several occasions (there is a dispute about precisely how many occasions). Where there is apparently less dispute is that the bank didn't exert itself sufficiently in trying to dissuade the customer from his actions.[135]

» Regulators should be sympathetic to and encourage those bankers who truly seek to help and support their customers. Regulation such as 'Treating Customers Fairly', whilst well intentioned, can easily be interpreted in a rigid way by both the regulators and the banks themselves. The consequence can be that all customers tend to be treated at the same mediocre level rather than each customer being treated in an appropriate and excellent way. Anti-money laundering legislation, introduced mainly to prevent illegal international movements of money, is often used an excuse to tie innocent, domestic customers in a welter of red tape.

» Much greater stress ought to be put on technical banking training, so that bankers fully understand the customer's problems and can be sympathetic to them. Far too many bank staff (though by no means all) have too little technical training to be fully confident when dealing with customers' problems. In addition, banking training should stress the particular responsibilities which attend being a banker.

» A similar point applies to bank boards. No one should expect bank directors to understand in detail all the complex derivatives in which their bank trades. But there is no excuse for directors failing to understand in detail the assumptions on which trading is based. Far too often, bank directors have been 'surprised' by outcomes which could reasonably have been expected given the circumstances. For example, too many boards have put reliance on the VAR (value at risk) measure as the main or only indicator of the risk being run. (see page 64)

» Relationship managers must be more than salespeople. This comment applies particularly in corporate banking. As detailed on page 36 the growth in credit departments in the seventies and eighties led to the responsibility for credit being removed in whole or part from the banks' relationship managers. The (perhaps predictable) result was that often relationship managers became, in effect, glorified sales executives. They had little reason to care too much about the creditworthiness of their customers and instead all too often tried to persuade them to take products which were unsuitable and sometimes dangerous. Relationship managers should resume joint responsibility for credit with the credit departments themselves and both groups should be rewarded in part in accordance with the credit quality of the lending book.

» The question arises, 'Should the above provisions be applied both to 'ring-fenced' and 'non ring-fenced' banks, as defined by the Vickers Report[136]. One of the major reasons I have adduced for bankers having obligations over and above those of other organisations is that if they get into trouble, they would be rescued. If the 'non ring-fenced banks' would not be rescued in these circumstances, why should they have obligations (legal or moral) greater than other commercial organisations? I think that there are two answers to this question. The first is that the behaviour I have recommended is that which is consistent with the proper behaviour of any commercial organisation (though the specific recommendations are obviously directed to the boards of banks). The moral suasion argument should therefore be directed at all banks, whether ring fenced or not. The second point is that all banks, 'ring-fenced' and other benefit directly or indirectly from the support which the ring-fenced banks will receive. While other non-banking organisations and individuals also benefit when government supports banks, it is the banking community itself which has the most to gain or lose.

If banks do change in the ways described above, there would be no need for legislation. If they do not, then I believe that banks should be forced to recognise their obligations to stakeholders taken as a whole and that these obligations should rank alongside, and not be subordinate to, the bank's obligation to maximise long-term shareholder value. It may only be necessary to apply these restrictions to a very limited number of banks, namely the 11 UK clearing banks. Of these,[137] just four, i.e. HSBC, Barclays, Royal Bank of Scotland and Lloyds Banking Group, have a stranglehold on the market. Between them, they hold around three quarters of personal accounts and a higher proportion of business accounts. Any legislation affecting the clearing banks would clearly affect the vast proportion of the market and could soon have a 'trickle down' effect on the smaller market participants. Alternatively, it may be felt necessary that all banks should be subject to a similar regime. Either way, the introduction of legislation would be a clear signal that the banks were incapable of internal reform. It would be much better if the banks were willing and able to transform themselves.

Conclusion

Clearly it is not possible to reconstruct banking behaviour *a la* 1958, even if it were desirable to do so. Society then was deferential: a hint from the Bank of England was enough to precipitate a change, while now banks will ask for the detail of the regulation before altering their behaviour and may contest it. Furthermore, the banking system was riddled with price fixing agreements and other non-competitive practices which happily have been largely swept away. Such cartels have not totally disappeared – witness the LIBOR fixing scandal – but they are much less widespread than they once were. And while prejudices against women, minority groups and others still exist within banking, they are not nearly as widespread as in the past, when banking was largely carried out by and for middle class men and their families.

Bankers in the twenty first century have to compete with highly professional counterparts worldwide and are expected to perform in very competitive environments. How can they be encouraged to do so while acting in a virtuous way as responsible members of society? The larger banks enjoy support from the state if they fail; how do they respond and show that they deserve this safety net?

I have tried to trace the ways in which bankers have lost touch with their customers and I believe that a key element in the rehabilitation of bankers is the reinstatement of a productive relationship between banker and customer. Central to this is a recognition that the banker/customer relationship is fundamentally different from many other supplier/customer relationships. Many customers do not fully understand the financial products they are using and are necessarily put in a situation where they have to trust their banker. If that trust is broken, the customer feels betrayed. That feeling is not very different if the banker has been accidently proved wrong about a product, service or market; negligent or guilty of misconduct (and there have been too many instances of each in recent years). In all these circumstances the customer feels let down.

A better attitude towards customers will not automatically cure all the problems of the banking sector. (It will not, of course, stop mistakes being made, though it will reduce the number of these instances and the way in which the mistake is dealt with will again demonstrate the banker's true customer care.) An approach which puts the customer first and treats each customer in a way in which the banker him or herself would like to be treated will, I think, have a profound and positive effect.

What is clear is that the regulators' attempts to introduce 'Treating Customers Fairly' behaviour does not begin to address the problem, because it seeks to ensure that different customers are treated in similar and satisfactory ways, not that all customers are treated excellently. Because all customers differ, a really good banker might feel that the solution to the same problem may be different for two apparently similar customers. It is important that regulation does not impede good bankers from taking these – in the best sense – discriminatory decisions.

Another strand is the fearsome complexity which bank boards and executives face. I have noted above that, while many bank directors are intelligent and hard-working, I am doubtful that many understand enough about some of the newer products which their banks trade. In particular, I think that there has been insufficient debate on the assumptions which underlie these trades. Training for board membership should include developing skills in asking the appropriate questions about complex products which the directors probably will never fully understand in detail. Equally, there should be more formal vocational training of bankers. Over the last few decades, banks have employed a smaller percentage of people with 'Institute of Bankers' qualifications and more very bright people from good universities with little, if any, formal banking training. It was generally assumed that these bright people would learn about banking 'on the job'. While there is some justification for this thought, I wonder whether bankers might not benefit from more formal training in their craft, and in particular, some greater long-term perspective on the risks involved in financial services. Even if such improvements take place, it is a moot point whether universal banks are just too complicated for boards to manage. Professor Julian Franks told the Parliamentary Commission on Banking Standards:

That adds to my view that banks are complex and if you think that you can fix boards to fix these problems, that is a great mistake. You need structural changes. We can improve boards, but do not lay too much emphasis on that as a way of stopping the problem [...].[138]

A final strand is that banks should wake up and realise that they are not like other commercial organisations. Banks are favourably treated by society because a failure by a major bank would have catastrophic consequences. They can rely on liquidity support from the Bank of England and (it appears) shareholder support from the government if the problems cannot be solved by short-term lending. No other type of commercial organisation enjoys these privileges. In return, banks and their boards should respond by being held to high community standards.

It is hoped that the bankers themselves will take these tasks in hand and put their own houses in order, to improve customer service, simplify their businesses and formalise their banking education, so that risks can be kept under control. I have made some suggestions on how this may be achieved. In the event that the bankers disappoint, I think it may be helpful for the government to have some kind of change in law or regulation up its sleeve. A toughening of the provisions under Section 172 of the Companies Act may be necessary. Bank boards could be required to take into account the interests of customers and other stakeholders alongside their obligation to maximise long-term shareholder value. When the two aims conflict, the board's responsibility would be to balance these conflicting interests. Boards are — or should be — used to such balancing acts.

Whether legislation or practice changes, it is clear is that, despite some recent improvements, the bankers still have a long way to go before they can claim to have recovered their role as 'a placid, safe centre to financial Britain'.

THE END[139]

NOTES

[1] Sampson, Anthony The Anatomy of Britain.
  Harper and Row 1962 p.373

[2] The Radcliffe Report: A Short Guide National Institute of
  Economic and Social Research 1959, 5(1) p.18

[3] Sampson, Anthony The Anatomy of Britain.
  Harper and Row 1962 p.365

[4] Ferguson, Niall The Ascent of Money.
  Penguin Books 2009 p.56

[5] Sampson, Anthony The Anatomy of Britain.
  Harper and Row 1962 p.371

[6] Sampson, Anthony The Anatomy of Britain.
  Harper and Row 1962 p.370.
  As at December 31, 1961 the London joint stock banks held
  38.8% of their assets in Cash, Treasury and other bills, Money
  at call or short notice and Deposits at the Bank of England.

[7] Banerjee, Ryan N and Mio, Hitoshi Bank of England Staff
  Working Paper No. 536 The impact of liquidity regulation
  on banks.
  July 2015 p. 35.

[8] Sampson, Anthony The Anatomy of Britain.
  Harper and Row 1962 p.373

[9] In 1975, the earliest year for which I could find data, building
  society deposits were £ 22.5 billion, compared to £ 19.2
  billion total bank deposits. Source.
  ONS Financial Statistics.

[10] Sampson, Anthony The Anatomy of Britain.
  Harper and Row 1962 p.376

[11] ibid. p.371

[12] While it is difficult to obtain perfect comparisons of bankers' remuneration over the last half century, the following may be a guide. In 1962, Anthony Sampson (The Anatomy of Britain p. 17) noted that there were 3000 people throughout British society with salaries over £ 20,000 p.a., equivalent in inflation adjusted terms (but not salary adjusted terms) to around £ 400,000 p.a. today. It is not clear how many of these were bankers. On Wednesday 30 March, Julia Kollewe and Bob Davies in the Guardian online reported that there were around 3000 bankers in the UK earning over £ 800,000 p.a. Given that bonuses were much less prevalent in the 1950s and 1960s, there is evidence that bankers relative remuneration is now much higher than 50 years ago.

[13] Zawadzki, KKF 'Competition and Credit Control' Basil Blackwell Oxford 1981 p. 127

[14] Pierce, David G and Tysome, Peter J 'Monetary Economics: Theories, Evidence and Policy' Butterworth-Heinemann 1980 p. 270

[15] Davies, Richard; Richardson, Peter; Katinaite, Vaiva; and Manning, Mark 'Evolution of the UK banking system' Bank of England Quarterly Bulletin 2010 Q4. P.322

[16] Bank for International Settlements Quarterly Press Release on International Banking Developments (June 1979) Size of Eurocurrency markets net of double counting due to interbank positions. As quoted in Lomax, David and Gutmann, PTG The Euromarkets and International Financial Policies MacMillan 1981

[17] Schenk, Catherine Crisis and Opportunity: The Policy Environment of International Banking in the City of London, 1958–1980. in ed. Cassis, Youssef and Bussiere, Eric London and Paris as International Financial Centres in the Twentieth Century Oxford University Press 2005 p.212

[18] 50th Anniversary of the Eurobond Market International Capital Market Association (ICMA) http://www.icmagroup.org/About-ICMA/Organisation/

history/50th-anniversary-of-the-eurobond-market/
Accessed 14 December 2016

[19] Examples in this and next paragraph are based on a BBC Radio 4 programme 'The Plastic Revolution' broadcast on Monday 29 August 2016 at 11.00 a.m.

[20] Zawadzki, KKF Competition and Credit Control Basil Blackwell Oxford 1981 p.33

[21] ibid. p,153

[22] https://en.wikipedia.org/wiki/Secondary_banking_crisis_of_1973%E2%80%9375 Wikipedia Secondary banking crisis of 1973–75.
Accessed 14 December 2016

[23] Reid, Margaret. The Secondary Banking Crisis, 1973–75: Its Causes and Course. Macmillan, London (1982)/ 2nd ed, Hindsight, London (2003) ISBN 978-0-9541567- p.192

[24] Capie, Forrest The Bank of England: 1950s to 1979 Cambridge University Press 2012 p.363

[25] Gadanecz, Blaise The syndicated loan market: structure, development and implications BIS Quarterly Review December 2004 p76

[26] And named after him.

[27] Terry, Brian J The International Handbook of Corporate Finance The Chartered Institute of Bankers 1997 p.266 et seq.

[28] Dennis, S and Mullineaux D (2000): "Syndicated loans", Journal of Financial Intermediation, vol 9, October 2000 pp 404–26.

[29] For a description of the Herstatt Bank crisis see, for example, 'Bank Failures in Mature Economies' Basel Committee on Banking Supervision Working Paper No. 13 April 2004 pp. 4-6

[30] Rebroadcast on BBC Radio 4 programme 'The Plastic Revolution' on Monday 29 August 2016 at 11.00 a.m. The Bank Manager's name was Neville Tarrett (sp?)

[31] 'Developments in UK Banking and monetary statistics since the Radcliffe Report. Bank of England Quarterly Bulletin September 1985 pp. 392 et seq.

[32] www.economist.com/node/3598768 27 January 2005.
Accessed 17 December 2016

[33] 'Over the Counter' i.e. trading between two parties without
the intervention of an exchange

[34] Derivatives Statistics– Bank for International Settlements
www.bis.org/statistics/derstats.htm
Accessed 27 December 2016

[35] https://www.johnkay.com/2015/06/15/
other-peoples-money-introduction/.
Accessed 18 January 2017.
Professor Kay's reference to Humbert Wolfe is taken from
that writer's The Uncelestial City, *1930*

[36] As noted in https://en.wikipedia.org/wiki/Big_Bang_
(Accessed 1 July 2017)
Big Bang resulted from an agreement by the Thatcher
Government and the London Stock Exchange, settling a
long-term anti-trust case between the Stock Exchange and
the Office of Fair Trading under the Restrictive Trade
Practices Act 1956.

[37] http://www.tradingeconomics.com/united-kingdom/
households-debt-to-gdp.
Accessed 30 May 2017

[38] http://www.dailymail.co.uk/news/article-2891048/
Thatcher-warned-Big-Bang-reform-City-create-bubble-
pricked-unscrupulous-bankers.html#ixzz3lAYNNeG0.
Accessed 1 July 2017

[39] As noted on page 2, stock jobbers 'made markets' in shares and
bonds, dealing only with each other and with stock brokers.
Brokers were the intermediaries between the jobbers and the
customers (personal, corporate and institutional). They did
not run positions in shares and bonds.

[40] ISDA Market Surveys 1985–2010

[41] Of which approximately 75% was estimated to have been
denominated in US dollars,
https://en.wikipedia.org/wiki/Eurodollar.
Accessed 25 January 2017

[42] Wake, Jehanne 'Kleinwort, Benson:
The History of Two Families in Banking'
Oxford University Press 1997

[43] Augar, Philip 'The Death of Gentlemanly Capitalism'
Penguin Books 2000

[44] http://www.riskencyclopedia.com/articles/barings_debacle/
Accessed 29 October 2015

[45] A process which could not have continued for ever.

[46] Augar, Philip 'The Death of Gentlemanly Capitalism'
Penguin Books 2000 p. 109

[47] ibid. p. 109, quoting Lorenz, Andrew 'BZW: The first ten
years' BZW London 1996, p.35

[48] Barclays Bank Plc Annual Report and Accounts 1992 p.79.
Figures are for UK Domestic Bank, not UK Banking
Services

[49] Barclays plc Annual Report and Accounts 1994 p.14

[50] Barclays plc Annual Report and Accounts 1997 p.12
BZW includes Barclays Capital and Former BZW
businesses.
UK Banking Services includes Life Fund Charge and
Write-down of leases

[51] https://en.wikipedia.org/wiki/Goldman_Sachs
(accessed 1 November 2017)

[52] Select Committee on Treasury 'Ninth Special Report'
published 27 July 1999
http://www.publications.parliament.uk/pa/cm199899/
cmselect/cmtreasy/605/60502.htm Paragraph 5
Accessed 27 January 2017.

[53] Government's Response to the Treasury 'Ninth Special
Report', dated 22 October 1999.
http://www.publications.parliament.uk/pa/cm199899/
cmselect/cmtreasy/880/88003.htm.
Accessed 27 January 2017

[54] Tayler, Graham 'UK Building Society demutualisation
motives' Business Ethics Volume 12 Number 4 October 2003
pp. 394–402

[55] According to the Building Societies Association website
https://www.bsa.org.uk/
Accessed 25 January 2017

[56] https://en.wikipedia.org/wiki/Building_society
Accessed 3 July 2017

[57] http://news.bbc.co.uk/1/hi/business/7641925.stm
Accessed 2 July 2017

[58] Derived from https://www.statista.com/statistics/386938/
uk-banks-branches-number/
Accessed 3 July 2017

[59] French, Shaun Leyshon, Andrew and Meek, Sam The
Changing Geography of British Bank and Building Society
Branch Networks,
2003–2012. School of Geography,
University of Nottingham, NG7 2RD

[60] Stiglitz, Joseph E 'Vanity Fair' January 2009 Paragraph
http://www.vanityfair.com/news/2009/01/stiglitz200901-2
Accessed 3 July 2017

[61] Rawlings P, Georgosouli , A and Russo , Costanza
'Regulation of financial services :Aims and Methods'.
Queen Mary, University of London April 2014

[62] Treasury Committee, First Report: Barings Bank and
International Regulation, HC 65, Sess.1996/97, para.24.
Quoted in Rawlings P, Georgosouli, A and Russo,
Costanza 'Regulation of financial services:
Aims and Methods'. Queen Mary, University of London
April 2014 Paragraph 1.4

[63] www.riskencyclopedia.com
https://www.glynholton.com/notes/barings_debacle/
Retrieved 27 January 2017

[64] The BBC 11 April 2011,
http://www.bbc.co.uk/news/business-1303201.
Accessed 11 July 2017

[65] Oliver Lodge 'A Review of the UK Banking Industry'
Centre for Policy Studies July 2002

[66] ibid. Foreword by Howard Flight

[67] The speech by Tony Blair is reported by Guardian, 26 May 2005 at http://www.theguardian.com/ politics/2005/may/26/speeches.media as quoted in Rawlings P, A Georgosouli, A and Russo, Costanza 'Regulation of financial services: Aims and Methods'. Queen Mary, University of London April 2014: Paragraph 1.5.4

[68] The Telegraph 'Banks turn a deaf ear to Cruickshank' 4 April 2001

[69] Reducing administrative burdens – effective inspection and enforcement (the Hampton Report) March 2005

[70] According to Wikipedia, (https://en.wikipedia.org/wiki/ Long-Term_Capital_Management. Accessed 11 July 2017) the banks who agreed to rescue LTCM were:
$ 300 million: Bankers Trust, Barclays, Chase, Credit Suisse First Boston, Deutsche Bank, Goldman Sachs, Merrill Lynch, J.P. Morgan, Morgan Stanley, Salomon Smith Barney, UBS
$ 125 million: Société Générale
$ 100 million: Paribas, Credit Agricole
Bear Stearns and Lehman Brothers declined to participate and, interestingly, were not rescued in the 2008 collapse.

[71] Bank of England Governor Thomson Hankey, quoted in Mervyn King, 'The End of Alchemy' Little, Brown 2016

[72] International Monetary Fund 'World Economic Outlook and International Capital Markets: Interim Assessment. December 1998 Chapter III: Turbulence in Mature Financial Markets' Box 3.4

[73] http://www.forbes.com/sites/eamonnfingleton/2013/09/15/ the-best-news-for-america-this-year-larry-summers-drops- out-of-fed-chairman-tussle/#1ab81fe85237
Retrieved 30 January 2017

[74] Anderson, David A Study e Guide for: Economics by Example ISBN 9780716769347. Accessed 11 July 2017

[75] David Miles http://voxeu.org/article/what-optimal-leverage-bank
27 April 2011 Retrieved 30 January 2017.
Sources (as quoted by David Miles): UK: Sheppard, D (1971), The growth and role of UK financial institutions 1880–1962, Methuen, London; Billings, M and Capie, F (2007), 'Capital in British banking', 1920–1970, Business History, Vol 49(2), pages 139–162; BBA, ONS published accounts and Bank calculations.
Notes: (as quoted by David Miles) (a) UK data on leverage use total assets over equity and reserves on a time-varying sample of banks, representing the majority of the UK banking system, in terms of assets. Prior to 1970 published accounts understated the true level of banks' capital because they did not include hidden reserves. The solid line adjusts for this. 2009 observation is from H1. (b) Change in UK accounting standards. (c) International Financial Reporting Standards (IFRS) were adopted for the end–2005 accounts. The end–2004 accounts were also restated on an IFRS basis. The switch from UK GAAP to IFRS reduced the capital ratio of the UK banks in the sample by approximately 1 percentage point in 2004.

[76] The Big Short, a 2015 American comedy-drama film directed by Adam McKay and written by McKay and Charles Randolph, based on Lewis, Michael The Big Short: Inside the Doomsday Machine' W W Norton & Co. 2010.

[77] Anderson, David e-Study Guide for:
Economics by Example
ISBN 9780716769347.
Accessed 11 July 2017

[78] There were other reasons for securitisation, for example booking accounting profits on sale and risk transfer.

[79] IMF International Financial Statistics as quoted in https://en.wikipedia.org/wiki/Reserve_requirement
Retrieved 31 January 2017

[80] I have not been able to find data which shows that average maturities have lengthened over the relevant period, but intuitively I believe this to have been the case.

[81] 'How a financial darling fell from grace, and why regulators didn't catch it'
The Economist Oct 18th 2007 | From the print edition

[82] 'The Failure of the Royal Bank of Scotland'
FSA Board Report p.27

[83] The BBC 11 April 2011, quoted in en.m.wikipedia.org Big Bang (financial markets)'
Retrieved 31 January 2017

[84] http://www.heraldscotland.com/news/12439228.Too_bad_I_never_got_fired_SIR_GEORGE_MATHEWSON.
Accessed 12 June 2017

[85] http://uk.businessinsider.com/why-rbs-failed-as-an-investment-bank-2015-3.
Accessed 12 June 2017

[86] Bank of England Quarterly Bulletin 2010 Q4
'Evolution of the UK Banking System' Richard Davies, Peter Richardson, Vaiva Katinaite and Mark Manning

[87] Parliamentary Commission on Banking Standards
'Changing Banking for Good' 2013 Paragraph 679
https://www.publications.parliament.uk/pa/jt201314/jtselect/jtpcbs/27/27ii09.htm
Accessed 14 July 2017

[88] ibid. Paragraph 1147

[89] ibid. Paragraph 1148

[90] http://www.thisismoney.co.uk/money/markets/article-2277167/You-impose-moral-standards-people-dont-wish-moral-Disgraced-ex-RBS-boss-blames-traders-Libor-scandal.html#ixzz44rkZXQx3

[91] Parliamentary Commission on Banking Standards
'Changing Banking for Good' 2013
Paragraphs 680 and 1149

[92] ibid. Paragraph 1151

[93] Bowers, Simon RBS collapse: the key players The Guardian Monday 12 December 2011

[94] Comprising a) Asset Protection Scheme £ 202 billion RBS; £ 255 billion Lloyds Banking Group b) Share Purchases

£ 46 billion RBS; £ 21 billion Lloyds Banking Group c) Contingent capital £ 8 billion RBS Source: National Audit Office 'Taxpayer support for UK Banks' Frequently Asked Questions. Last updated July 2016.

These figures ignore any benefit that RBS and Lloyds may have received from sector wide government support schemes.

[95] *Hosking, Patrick 'The Times' Wednesday 13 September 2016*

[96] Office of National Statistics

'Rest of the World holdings of UK shares by value'.

[97] Keynes, John Maynard 'Indian Currency and Finance' 1913. Chapter VI, Paragraph 40

[98] *Van der Weyer, Martin 'UK: Corrective Surgery' Management Today Published 01 August 1997 Last Updated 31 August 2010.* http://www.managementtoday.co.uk/ uk-corrective-surgery/article/410852.

[99] *Treanor, Jill 'PPI claims — all you need to know about the mis-selling scandal' theguardian.com 2 August 2016. Retrieved 5 February 2017.*

[100] Traditionally corporate finance advisors had 'clients' while lending bankers had 'customers'.

[101] Smith, Greg 'Why I Left Goldman Sachs: A Wall Street Story' Grand Central Publishing 2012

[102] The Washington Post 'Wonkblog' https://www.washingtonpost.com/news/wonk/wp/2012/ 10/10/the-truth-about-goldman-sachs-and-the-muppets/ Retrieved 25 September 2016

[103] *The Big Short,* a 2015 American comedy-drama film directed by Adam McKay and written by McKay and Charles Randolph, based on Lewis, Michael *The Big Short: Inside the Doomsday Machine'* W W Norton & Co. 2010.

[104] House of Commons Treasury Committee '*The FSA's report into the failure of RBS*' Fifth Report of Session 2012–13. 16 October 2012 page 3.

[105] Kar-Gupta, Sudip and Le Guernigou, Yann 'BNP freezes $ 2.2 bln of funds over subprime.' Reuters 9 August 2007.

[106] Jackson, Christopher and Sim, Mathew *'Recent developments in the sterling overnight money market.* Source: Bank of England Quarterly Bulletin Q3 2013 pp. 223–232

[107] 'Northern Rock to be Nationalised' BBC News 17 February 2008.

[108] House of Commons Treasury Committee *'The FSA's report into the failure of RBS'* Fifth Report of Session 2012–13. 16 October 2012 pages 8 and 9.

[109] The Financial Services Authority *The failure of the Royal Bank of Scotland* December 2011 page.7.

[110] Under this scheme Banks were able to borrow gilt edged securities (which could be easily sold) against the security of certain illiquid assets, though significantly eligible assets did NOT include US mortgages or derivative products.

[111] House of Commons Treasury Committee *'The FSA's report into the failure of RBS'* Fifth Report of Session 2012–13. 16 October 2012 page 9.

[112] The Telegraph Wilson, Harry Adrick, Philip and Ahmed, Kamal 11 December 2011. http://www.telegraph.co.uk/finance/newsbysector/ banksandfinance/8947559/RBS-investigation-Chapter-4- the-bail-out.html Accessed 14 August 2017.

[113] National Audit Office *'Taxpayer support for UK Banks' Frequently Asked Questions.* Last updated July 2016. These figures ignore any benefit that RBS and Lloyds may have received from sector wide government support schemes.

[114] The Financial Services Authority 'The failure of the Royal Bank of Scotland' December 2011 page 3.

[115] Bank of Scotland slammed by FSA for high-risk strategy https://www.theguardian.com/business/2012/mar/09/ bank-of-scotland-fsa-serious-misconduct. Accessed 14 August 2017.

[116] Moore claims that he was sacked by James Crosby, the Chief Executive because he raised concerns about risky lending.

[117] In some cases larger depositors were repaid as well.

[118] 'A review of corporate governance in UK banks and other financial industry entities' Final recommendations 26 November 2009.

[119] Financial Conduct Authority Press Releases. fca.org.uk.
Published: 07/07/2015
Last updated: 19/04/2016
Retrieved 5 February 2017

[120] Taylor, Martin 'The Fence and the Pendulum' Based on a speech given to the International Association of Credit Portfolio Managers, 22 May 2015. Bankofengland.co.uk.
Retrieved 5 February 2017

[121] Financial Services Authority as quoted by BBC News on 29 June 2012. Poor practices included
» Lack of clarity about the costs of stopping a product
» Failure to check whether the customer understood the risk
» Selling based on personal rewards rather than on the business needs

[122] https://www.stephensons.co.uk/site/businesses/.../interest_rate_swap_hedging/
Retrieved 13 October 2016

[123] National Audit Office 'Taxpayer support for UK Banks' Frequently Asked Questions.
Last updated July 2016.

[124] Brinded, Lianna 'The fired Barclays CEO had two nicknames inside the bank that tell you why he was forced out.'
Business Insider 8 July 2015 uk.businessinsider.com
Retrieved 6 February 2017.

[125] Of which I am a Liveryman.

[126] http://internationalbankers.org.uk/about-the-company/principles-for-good-business-conduct/accessed.
Retrieved 13 December 2016.

[127] Charkham, Jonathan 'Guidance for the Directors of Banks' Global Corporate Governance Forum. Focus 2.
The International Bank for Reconstruction and Development 2003. p. 25

[128] Parliamentary Commission on Banking Standards 'Changing Banking for Good' 2013 Paragraph 679.

[129] The Companies Act 2006, section 172 as quoted in Keay, Andrew 'The Duty to Promote the Success of the Company: is it Fit for Purpose?' School of Law, University of Leeds, 2010.

[130] Keay, Andrew 'The Duty to Promote the Success of the Company: is it Fit for Purpose?' School of Law, University of Leeds, 2010 Page 5.

[131] ibid. Page 19.

[132] Source: Google Finance.

[133] van der Weyer, Martin 'In this digital age, should we worry about bank branch closures? Yes, we should'. The Spectator 11 February 2017 Page 29.

[134] 'Money Box' BBC Radio 4. 11 February 2017

[135] Whatever the exact truth in this case, the story does I think ring true as the way in which many bankers currently behave.

[136] Vickers, John 'The Independent Commission on Banking' September 2011.

[137] Bank of England, Bank of Scotland, Barclays, Clydesdale Bank, The Co-operative Bank, HSBC Bank, Lloyds Bank, National Westminster Bank, Nationwide Building Society, The Royal Bank of Scotland and Santander UK.

[138] Parliamentary Commission on Banking Standards 'Changing Banking for Good' 2013 Paragraph 679.

[139] Parts of this piece first appeared in Peacock, Ian 'The raw winds of Change' Financial World October/November 2016 page 64.

Acknowledgements

I should first of all like to acknowledge all I have learnt from those colleagues with and for whom I have worked over the years. This book has stressed what has gone wrong with the banking system. I have not devoted much space to the bright, professional and ethical people who have worked and continue to work in the sector. I have been lucky perhaps, in working with many such people and I hope to have learnt a lot from them.

Thanks are also due to all those who have read the manuscript and have commented on the content, style and punctuation. They include Mark Burnyeat, Roy Eales, Sally Floyer, Shelley Gregory-Jones, Pete Hahn, Bill Hall, Tim Hindle, Alexander Hoare, David and Susan Kennett, Robert Ottley, Aly Peacock, Chris and Liz Peacock, John Shield, Keith Sykes, Corinne Urban, Piers Williamson and Ron Zimmern. They have improved the end result greatly, but the remaining errors of fact and style are mine.

I should also like to thank Bianca Pritz at Novum Publishing for providing the opportunity for a new author and for their invaluable help and guidance.

Born in Bristol in 1947, Ian Peacock
has already written several articles
for financial magazines and is now
publishing his first book,
'Bankers: From Pillars to Pariahs'.
Ian has had a long and varied career
in banking, commerce and charities.
He worked as a banker in London,
New York and Hong Kong and was a special
adviser to the Bank of England from 1998–2000.
He was also chairman of Mothercare, Howden
Joinery and the Westminster Abbey Finance
Advisory Committee. He lives in London with his
wife and enjoys travel, gardening and music in his
spare time.
He is a Quondam Fellow of Hughes Hall,
Cambridge.

The publisher

*He who stops
getting better
stops being good.*

This is the motto of novum publishing, and our focus
is on finding new manuscripts, publishing them and
offering long-term support to the authors.
Our publishing house was founded in 1997, and since
then it has become THE expert for new authors and
has won numerous awards.

**Our editorial team will peruse each manuscript
within a few weeks free of charge and without
obligation.**

You will find more information about
novum publishing and our books on the internet:

www.novum-publishing.co.uk

Printed in Poland
by Amazon Fulfillment
Poland Sp. z o.o., Wrocław